Ammi
an expression of love...

From the kitchen of my mother
NIRMALA PANDARINATHAN
Compiled and photographed by **Prasanna Pandarinathan**

an expression of love...

RUPA

Published by Rupa Publications India Pvt. Ltd 2022
7/16, Ansari Road, Daryaganj
New Delhi 110002

Sales Centres:
Allahabad Bengaluru Chennai
Hyderabad Jaipur Kathmandu
Kolkata Mumbai

Text and photograph copyright © Pressy Pandarinathan 2022

Background design on page 21: GarryKillian / Freepik.com
Photographs on pages 283, 292, 294: Freepik.com

Cover photograph: Sam Mohan
Author photograph: Abhishek Srivastava.

The views and opinions expressed in this book are the author's own and the facts are as reported by her which have been verified to the extent possible, and the publishers are not in any way liable for the same.

All rights reserved.

No part of this publication may be reproduced, transmitted, or stored in a retrieval system, in any form or by any means, electronic, mechanical, photocopying, recording or otherwise, without the prior permission of the publisher.

ISBN: 978-93-5520-297-0

First impression 2022

10 9 8 7 6 5 4 3 2 1

Printed by Lustra Print Process Pvt. Ltd, New Delhi

The moral right of the author has been asserted.

This book is sold subject to the condition that it shall not, by way of trade or otherwise, be lent, resold, hired out, or otherwise circulated, without the publisher's prior consent, in any form of binding or cover other than that in which it is published.

Food Photography by **Pressy Nathan** | Book Design by **Sheetal Parakh**

*In memory of our mother, Nirmala Pandarinathan,
for whom cooking was an expression of love!*

VEGETABLES 25

EGGS 59

POULTRY 73

MEATS 99

BAKES, ROASTS & GRILLS 187

SEAFOOD 137

PICKLES & CHUTNEYS 237

RICE & NOODLES 211

DESSERTS 267

PREFACE..17
NIRMALA PANDARINATHAN: AN INTRODUCTION..............19

VEGETABLES..25

Yam Fries..28
Sweet Mango Pachadi...31
Sundal..32
Eggplant and Drumsticks...35
Bitter Gourd Masala...36
Lentil Dumplings in Coconut Gravy...........................39
Banana Blossom Vadas...40
Steamed Lentil Balls in Tamarind Gravy....................43
Spicy Mango Pachadi..44
Black Lentil And Raw Banana....................................47
Stuffed Eggplants..49
Tamarind Curry with Baby Onions.............................50
Tangy Mixed Vegetables..52
Yam Curry..55

EGGS...59

Mom's Egg Curry...62
Egg Sambal..65
Stuffed Egg Cutlets..66
Eggs Stuffed with Cottage Cheese............................67
Egg Curry...69

POULTRY...73

Chicken Kurma...77
Mom's Chicken Curry...78
Tanjore Chicken Pepper Fry.................................81
Chettinad Chicken Curry.....................................84
Chicken in Cashew Curry....................................87
Singapore Ayam Panggang Chicken 88
Roti Jala...90
Chicken in Curry Leaves and Nuts.....................93
Lankan Chicken Curry...94

MEAT..99

Mutton Pepper Fry...102
Lamb Chops...104
Mutton with Gongura Leaves...........................107
Minced Mutton Cutlets......................................109
Kari Keema Kembing...110
Mutton Brain Seekh...111
Pepper Masala Mutton Chops..........................113
Irish Stew..114
Trotters Stew..117
Minced Meatball Curry......................................118
Mutton Kurma..121
Traditional South Indian Mutton Curry.............122
Mutton Dalcha...124
Brain Omelette...126
Mutton Stew...127
Fried Meatballs— Kolla Urandai........................129
Liver Fry..130
Boneless Lamb Fry..133

SEAFOOD	**137**
Fish Curry	142
Chettinad Fish Fry	145
Steamed Fish in Banana Leaves	146
Pamban Fish Curry	149
Fish Sambal	152
Tamarind Fish Curry	153
Stuffed Fish Masala	156
Fish Curry in Coconut Milk	159
Dried Fish Poriyal	160
Fish Puttu with Moringa Leaves	161
Prawns and Green Peas Masala	164
Prawn Curry	166
Spicy Prawn Masala	168
Prawn Kurma	170
Goong Pad—Fried Prawns	171
Prawns in Theeyal Masala	172
Spicy Chilli Crab	175
Singapore-style Spicy Crab Curry	176
Crab Meat Puttu	177
Stuffed Crab Shells	179
Crab Masala	180
Squid Masala	182

BAKES, ROASTS AND GRILS...187

Grilled Orange Chicken...192
Roast Chicken..194
Bell Peppers Stuffed with Mince.......................................197
Stuffed Baked Tomatoes..198
Baked Cauliflower in White Sauce...................................200
Mom's Shepherd's Pie...203
Cheese Stuffed Bell Peppers..204
Old English Casserole..206
Stuffed Roast Chicken..207

RICE AND NOODLES...211

Layered Mutton Dum Biryani..216
Sofiyani Chicken Biryani..218
Raw Mango Yoghurt Rice...219
Prawn Biryani..220
Coconut Rice...223
Tamarind Rice...225
Green Masala Biryani..226
Classic Ambur-style Biryani..229
Noodles and Veggies in Coconut Sauce.......................230
Chicken and Prawn Noodles..233
Soba Noodles...234

PICKLES AND CHUTNEYS 237

Eggplant Pickle.. 242
Green Chilli Pickle in Mustard Oil..................................... 243
Fish Pickle.. 244
Fish Pickle in Mustard Oil... 246
Cauliflower, Carrot and Turnip Pickle.............................. 247
Shrimp Pickle 249
Spicy Chilli and Tomato Pickle... 250
Curry Leaves Chutney 253
Date and Apricot Chutney 256
Indian Gooseberry Pickle 259
Ridge Gourd Chutney 260

DESSERTS 267

Adhirasam.. 272
Black Rice Halwa... 274
Eggless Curd Cake... 275
Coconut Balls... 276
Jackfruit Payasam.. 279
Black Rice Pudding.. 280
Date Cake.. 282
Semolina Balls 285
Poli—Stuffed Sweet Flatbread.. 286

SPICES, STOCKS AND MASALAS 288

MEMORIES OF NIRMALA.. 290
AFTERWORD... 293
ACKNOWLEDGEMENTS... 294

A recipe has no soul. You, as the cook, must bring soul to the recipe.

—Thomas Keller

Preface

The fragrance of fresh spices being ground in our kitchen each morning served as our alarm clock. I surfaced each morning to the slow, rhythmic sound of the grinding stone or *ammi* as it is called in Tamil, that Mom used for everyday cooking. She used the *ammi* as opposed to the mixer since the slow grinding of chutneys and the masalas on the stone brought out the flavours, oils and spice, combining them and giving them a beautiful soft texture simply not attainable by a machine.

Nowadays, when I wake up I sometimes lie in bed listening to the silence—a void that was left by her passing away. The *ammi* misses her too!

Eating at her well-laden and strategically placed table was like opening your heart to her! It was her way of watching you lovingly as you ate, letting you talk, coaxing you to try some of her baked crab shells, and you got up feeling light at heart but full of love, as if your woes had been replaced by a meal of hope.

Even when the tragic loss of my brother and her last-born gripped her in unspoken gloom, it was her deep bond with cooking and feeding others that brought back some of the light in her life. When I casually mentioned that I'd like to record her timeless recipes in a book so all of us have access to these, her large beautiful eyes lit up and she got busy penning these delightful culinary treasures from the different regions she'd lived in. Her last few years were spent in lovingly gathering and writing recipes, often taking us back to the beautiful garden of her home in Chennai; or by the bluest sea, bagging the best catch with the fishermen; or at the many homes she'd been to, narrating tales about her culinary journey, which inspired her art of soulful cooking.

Her entire repertoire of recipes spans South India, Ipoh, Penang, Singapore, Indonesia and Europe. This book contains some of these, which have been carefully selected by us—her family. These are mostly simple, home-styled and easy-to-cook, yet alive with the aromas, flavours and textures that she experienced during her extraordinary journey through life.

The recipes help us to bond and relive the beautiful and wholesome memories that we shared with her, making us believe how deeply food affects us, and in sharing them we hope you enjoy the warmth and joy that emanates from a repast of a perfectly glazed juicy roast chicken or a flavourful fish sambal that your family and friends have gathered over.

Here's to carrying on your tradition, Ma!

Nirmala Pandarinathan: An Introduction

This is my mother's story. Food holds a history for everyone, for my mom it began in the melting pot of culture and cuisines—Colonial Singapore. She was raised here in a mix of Indian, Malaysian, Chinese, Indonesian and Europian cultures. Born into a business Tamil family and the eldest of seven siblings, her childhood was spent in Singapore, and post boarding school, in Bangalore. At the age of nineteen due to our grandfather's ailing health it was decided to get our mother married. She met our father in Madras for whom it was love at first sight. They were married after a short courtship and she soon found herself in London where our father was completing his master's in Engineering at the Imperial College in London. Suddenly alone in a new country and an absolute novice in the kitchen, with time on her hands and the famous Cordon Bleu Cooking School close enough, she made her debut in the culinary art with continental cuisine. The French soups and freshly baked bread brought warmth to the cold English days and it was here that Mom's love affair with traditional French cuisine and its techniques began. Her newly learned art was experimented upon our dad, aunt and uncle.

The regular calls to her talented family cooks in Singapore ensured she picked up the little secrets of spicy Chettinad, Singaporean, Malay delicacies. Fuelled with her new passion, she soon found herself putting together a potpourri of simple and ingenious dishes for the family, displaying an inborn talent that even the cook came to rely on.

The saga of expressing love through cooking continued throughout her life and we, her family, were fortunate to experience that love waft into our lives each day. I am the fourth of the five siblings (four sisters and a brother) who took complete advantage of our mother's affection and loved her back dearly.

Mom and Dad brought us up not just nurturing us but everything around them with love. One of the objects of their affection was a charming farm in Madurai. Every morning Dad would be stationed at the portico of the house, on his favourite chair reading the newspaper and sipping a steaming cup of filter coffee. Mom seated next to him would be deftly chopping, dicing and slicing the vegetables she planned to use for the day. Their conversations ranged from tending to my mother's precious jasmines and tuberoses to discussions on the political state of the country and more. I would often stand by the doorway and watch them interact with love and mutual respect.

Over time, we left the nest one by one and her entrepreneurial side emerged. And one of her businesses was related to food, which naturally flourished. With the birth of her grandchildren, Anush, Sanjit and Avantika, all her attention, warmth and love was showered on them. It was now their turn to sample her culinary magic and build a wish list of their own.

From her extensive collection of recipes, she made everything from baked crabs to biryani. It was easy to understand why our brother's friends dubbed her the 'Best Mom' and why our home was an open house, where the aromas of whatever was being crafted in her kitchen first greeted visitors.

Shopping in local markets was always one of her guilty pleasures. Accompanying her to one was like taking a child to a candy store. Her eyes would twinkle at the very sight of fresh produce, varieties of meat and other local offerings.

When my mother passed away in 2010 we inherited a memoir of devotion and love, bound by priceless recipes. Watching her cook over the years, we came to realize that her relationship with food was all about unique experiences, magical moments and immeasurable grams of love. As you read on, you will also discover the many aspects of your relationship with food.

VEGETABLES

Vegetables of all colours packed with nutrients and cooked with flair were a major part of all our home-cooked meals. At school, my friends would eagerly wait for my lunch box to open for the variety of salads and vegetables that Mom packed neatly. Our brother, Pratap, was also a big reason why she loved to cook exotic vegetarian fare—he was, strangely, a complete vegetarian in our family. Even when he was just a toddler all attempts to feed him non-vegetarian food hidden in the folds of rotis or rice were in vain as he simply rejected them. And so Mom made peace and thus, the latter part of her life she started her very own organic vegetable garden which she had in our farm! From this haven came the freshest vegetables, fruits, bees and honey, and the sight of birds and nests. While most of the vegetables were used in her kitchen, the surplus would always be generously distributed amongst all the working hands at home and the farm. With so many happy hands working, the garden eventually blossomed into a large orchard. Mom, the entrepreneur, soon had enough produce to sell at the market and Dad would lovingly tease her that she was earning more from her cash crops than he was from the rest of the farm produce. Her creative spirit, entrepreneurial skill, generous heart, and gentle but persuasive manner made this farm a thriving oasis for birds, bees and people. She was also proud of the quality of vegetables her orchard produced—never compromising on that.

The garden, after her demise, lay in wait for tender hands to fill the void again and Dad expressed his wish to fill it up with Mom's favourite flowers. After driving around for hours, we found a nursery from where he picked tuberose, jasmine and other flower saplings to plant. Each time I visit, I watch him pluck roses and hibiscus from her garden and place them at Mom's altar. For being one who could never bare his emotions, this gesture never fails to move me deeply—I can see how much he misses his soulmate.

Let's dive through these simple recipes, made to delight every vegetarian—the way to one's heart, gastronomically speaking, is through the stomach!

YAM FRIES

My sister would hover about the kitchen when we had these crispy yams trying to get her hands on a few of them before the rest of us did. She would be shown out by Mom, but not without a plateful of fried yams and definitely not without a very pleased grin on her face.

PREP TIME: 15 MIN. | MARINATION TIME: 20 MIN. | COOKING TIME: 10 MIN. | SERVES: 4

500 gm yam
3 cups water
¼ tsp turmeric powder
3 tbsp chilli powder
1 tbsp pepper powder
a few curry leaves
2 cups oil
salt to taste

Slice the skin of the yam (apply oil on your palm first as this will reduce the itchiness).

Cut into ½ inch thick slices like French fries and cook in 2 cups of water for 8–10 minutes.

Remove the yam pieces from the water and set them aside to cool.

Mix all the dry powders, add salt and apply them to the yam.

Marinate the yam pieces for 20 minutes.

Heat the oil in a pan and shallow fry the pieces till golden brown. Add salt.

Add curry leaves to enhance the flavour.

SWEET MANGO PACHADI

A mix of yoghurt and chopped salad vegetables is what a pachadi really is but this dish is a different take, featuring the king of fruits in its raw form.

PREP TIME: 120 MIN. | COOKING TIME: 30 MIN. | SERVES: 4

2 cups chopped raw (green) mango
½ cup powdered jaggery
1 tsp rice flour mixed with 3 tsp water
¼ tsp turmeric powder
salt to taste

For Tempering
1 tsp mustard seeds
2 red chillies
a few curry leaves
a pinch of asafoetida
2 tsp oil

Heat the jaggery till it thickens, then strain and put aside.
Wash the raw mango well. Trim the edges and chop it into cubes. Discard the seed.
Put the chopped mango in a pan of water till it is immersed.
Let it cook for a few minutes until the pieces soften. Add the jaggery syrup.
Let it cook for 5 minutes and simmer. Add salt.
When the mangoes are nicely blended with the jaggery syrup, begin tempering simultaneously.
Heat the oil in a deep pan. Add the mustard seeds, red chillies, asafoetida and curry leaves till the ingredients begin to sputter. Take the pan off the fire and set it aside to cool.
Add the rice flour paste and let it boil on a slow flame for 2 minutes. Then add the tempering, mix well and take off the stove again.

Serve warm with rice and sambar.

SUNDAL

Sundal, usually prepared as naivedyam (an offering), takes us down the memory lane of our days in Chennai, most of which were spent on the beach and in the markets. A stroll down past the famous Marina Beach would take us to the hawkers selling sundal in wicker baskets, which we ate by the sea while watching the sunset. Those days hold another memory—whenever my mother with her almond eyes and dancer looks walked down the market, people would stop and ask her if she was 'that famous actress' from the South Indian movies. Mom would blush and thank them for the compliment.

PREP TIME: OVERNIGHT | COOKING TIME: 30 MIN. | SERVES: 4

250 gm black or white chickpeas
1 onion
¼ cup coconut flakes
5 dry red chillies
2 tsp oil
1 tsp mustard seeds
a few curry leaves
salt to taste

Wash and soak the chickpeas overnight and pressure cook for 4–5 whistles. Drain the water and set aside the chickpeas.

Chop the onions and break the dry red chillies into small pieces.

Pour the oil in a deep frying pan and fry the mustard seeds and curry leaves.

Add the onions and dry red chillies, sauté till light brown. Add the chickpeas to the pan and mix well.

Garnish with coconut flakes.

EGGPLANT AND DRUMSTICKS

Fresh produce makes all the difference to a dish, so we made trips (sometimes more than once a day) to the local market with Mom just to get fresh vegetables. She would joke with the vendors and distribute candies to their children, while her nimble fingers picked out green drumsticks.

PREP TIME: 15 MIN. | COOKING TIME: 20 MIN. | SERVES: 4–6

500 gm eggplant	Peel and cut the eggplants into long strips and soak them in salt water.
6 drumsticks	Cut the drumsticks into 2–3 inch pieces.
1 onion	Slice the onions and chop the tomatoes finely.
3 tomatoes	Pour the oil in a deep frying pan, add the onions and stir fry till golden brown, then add tomatoes, ginger and garlic paste and stir for a few minutes.
¼ cup coconut milk	
1 tbsp chilli powder	
1 tsp garlic paste	
1 tsp ginger paste	Mix chilli powder, salt and turmeric powder, then coat the drumsticks with the powder.
2 tbsp oil	
¼ tsp turmeric powder	Cook the drumsticks till half cooked.
salt to taste	Then add the eggplants, coconut milk, stir well and cook on slow flame till it is semi-dry.

Note:
Eggplants can be substituted for potatoes or Lima beans.

BITTER GOURD MASALA

As kids we were pretty reluctant to eat this dish, but we soon started relishing it as bitter gourd is an acquired taste. When it is cooked with green mango and coconut, the vegetable is anything but bitter.

PREP TIME: 10 MIN. | COOKING TIME: 15 MIN. | SERVES: 4

250 gm bitter gourd
2 tsp grated ginger
4 tsp coconut flakes
2 tsp coriander powder
2 tsp aniseed powder
2 tsp grated green mango
1 tsp garam masala
3 tsp oil
3 green chillies
a few curry leaves
a few coriander leaves
salt to taste

Scrape the outer skin of each bitter gourd, make a cut lengthwise, rub salt over it, leave for 2 hours.

Wash the salted bitter gourd and chop the chillies.

Mix the green chillies, grated ginger and coconut flakes, aniseed, coriander powder, garam masala and grated mango well.

Fill each gourd with the mix.

Tie it with a thread and shallow fry the stuffed bitter gourds on low flame till golden brown. Cover and cook till done.

LENTIL DUMPLINGS IN COCONUT GRAVY

Dumplings made of mixed lentils in coconut gravy make a wholesome dish and are a great source of protein.

PREP TIME: 15 MIN. | COOKING TIME: 25 MIN. | SERVES: 4–6

100 gm black lentil
100 gm Bengal gram
20 gm green gram
1 tsp carom seeds
1 tsp baking soda
3 tsp oil
4 green chillies
salt to taste

For Gravy
2 onions
2 cups tomato puree
1 cup water
1 tbsp garlic paste
2 cups coconut milk
1–2 tbsp red chilli powder
(depending on taste)

For Seasoning
1 tsp mustard seeds
1 tsp black lentil (urad dal)
2 tbsp oil
a few curry leaves

Soak the dals overnight and grind them to a paste. Add baking soda and salt to the paste and mix well. Roll the paste into little dumplings. Heat oil and fry medium-sized dumplings on medium flame. Set aside.

For Gravy

Mince the onions, fry till golden brown and grind to a paste. Heat the oil in a pan, add the onion paste, garlic paste, tomato puree and chilli powder.

Add water, bring to a boil and add coconut milk. Boil for 10 minutes. Place the dumplings in a serving bowl and pour the gravy over them.

For Seasoning

Heat the oil. Add mustard seeds, black lentil and curry leaves. Pour over the gravy in the bowl.

Serve with rice.

BANANA BLOSSOM VADAS

High in fibre, the banana blossom vadas are crispy on the outside and tender on the inside. A simple way to ensure the vadas turn out sweet and not bitter is to open the outer maroon shell of the blossom and check whether the flowers within are pale yellow and not dark pink.

PREP TIME: 45 MIN. | COOKING TIME: 15 MIN. | SERVES: 4–6

2 banana flowers (whole)
6 green chillies
5 onions
3 tbsp garlic
4 tbsp curd
¼ tsp turmeric powder
3 tsp cumin powder
2 cups Bengal gram
100 gm roasted Bengal gram
a few coriander leaves (optional)
1 pinch asafoetida
a few curry leaves
1 small piece ginger
3 cups sesame oil
Salt to taste

Cleaning the Banana Blossoms

Rub oil on your hands and the cutting board to avoid staining them.
In a bowl add 2 cups of water and mix with 4–5 tbsp of curd and a tsp of turmeric and set aside.
Open the outer leaf and detach the pale yellow flowers. Remove all the layers and gather the flowers.
Pick a flower, pull the feathery plastic-like petal back and discard. Now observe the long matchstick-like stem inside the flower and remove that too. Both these (tepal and stigma) have to be removed carefully from each flower otherwise the vada will be bitter and hard.
Finely cut the flowers and soak them in the curd and turmeric mixture for 20 minutes to avoid discoloration.

Method

Wash and soak the Bengal gram for 3 hours and then drain it and set aside.
Drain the soaked banana blossoms.
Chop the onions, garlic and green chillies finely.
Wash and chop the curry and coriander leaves and finely chop the ginger.
Grind the soaked Bengal gram with ginger and garlic into a rough paste.
Mix cumin powder, a little salt, chopped curry leaves, onions, coriander leaves, green chillies, banana flowers and asafoetida into the ground paste.
Add salt to taste. Make small balls and flatten.
Deep fry the balls in sesame oil till golden brown.

Serve hot.

STEAMED LENTIL BALLS IN TAMARIND GRAVY

This is a quintessential South Indian dish bursting with spice and tanginess and is one of my favourites.

PREP TIME: 10 MIN. | COOKING TIME: 45 MIN. | SERVES: 4–6

2 tsp oil	Soak the Bengal gram in water for 30 minutes. Drain the water and then grind to a paste without adding water.
¼ kg Bengal gram	
½ tsp turmeric powder	Add salt and mix well, then roll into small lemon-sized balls and steam them in a steamer (idli steamer will do).
1 tsp chilli powder	
2 cups water	Grind the grated coconut flakes to a smooth paste.
a few cloves and cardamoms	Fry the onions, curry leaves, 4 slit green chillies, 1 finely chopped tomato, cardamoms, cloves, turmeric and coriander powder.
½ cup grated coconut	
finely chopped onions	Add water and coconut paste; boil for about 10 minutes and then simmer till the gravy is semi-thick. Add the steamed balls and boil for another 10 minutes.
4 green chillies	
1½ tbsp coriander powder	
1 tomato	Garnish with coriander leaves.
a few coriander leaves	
a few curry leaves	
salt to taste	

SPICY MANGO PACHADI

When the king of fruits makes its grand entry in the summer season we eagerly try out all the dishes that can have this delicious fruit. This dish could be the cousin of the traditional sweet mango pachadi and goes well with steamed rice.

COOKING TIME: 30 MIN. | SERVES: 4

2 medium ripe mangoes
5 green chillies
1 coconut grated
10 curry leaves
2 cups beaten yoghurt
½ tsp turmeric powder
½ tsp chilli powder
2 tsp raw soaked rice
2 tsp sesame oil
2 tsp cumin seeds
½ tsp mustard seeds
½ tsp salt

Wash and peel the mangoes. Cut them into long strips.

Grind the coconut, the green chillies and the soaked rice into a fine paste.

Heat the oil, add mustard seeds, cumin and curry leaves. Sauté well.

Add the paste and let it simmer till the consistency thickens.

Add the mangoes, turmeric, chilli powder and salt.

Mix well, add the beaten yoghurt and cook till soft.

BLACK LENTIL AND RAW BANANA

If you're looking for a highly nutritious meal, look no further. Packed with vitamin C, potassium, manganese, high fibre and low in calories, plantain has been on the regular South Indian menu forever.

COOKING TIME: 30 MIN. | SERVES: 4–6

500 gm raw bananas
½ tsp black lentil (urad dal)
½ tsp mustard seeds
¼ tsp turmeric powder
2 tbsp sesame oil
¼ cup coconut flakes
2 onions
10 chillies
a few curry leaves
salt to taste

Peel and cut the bananas finely, cut the onions finely as well. Slit the chillies.

Fry the onions, mustard seeds, urad dal, green chillies and curry leaves.

Add the bananas and mix well with turmeric and salt, and cover for 10 minutes.

When cooked add the coconut flakes with the onions.

STUFFED EGGPLANT

These gently fried eggplants turned our stomachs into bottomless pits all for a greater share even when there was enough to go around. Many years later when I cooked it myself, I was surprised by the ease of preparing this dish.

PREP TIME: 10 MIN. | COOKING TIME: 20 MIN. | SERVES: 4

8 small eggplants
3 tbsp oil
a few coriander leaves

For Stuffing
grind the following:
1 tsp coriander powder
1 tsp chilli powder
1 tsp sugar
1 tsp mango powder
(or lemon juice)
¼ tsp fenugreek seeds
½ tsp turmeric powder
2 large onions
salt to taste

Wash and pat the eggplants dry.
Slit each into four lengthwise, keeping the stem.
Stuff them with the masala paste.
Heat the oil and cook on low flame.
Turn the eggplants carefully.
Cook till they are soft and tender.
Garnish with coriander leaves.

TAMARIND CURRY WITH BABY ONIONS

Simple, tangy and delicious, this recipe is from our grandmother who lived in Tanjore. Ma tweaked it using tamarind pulp instead of tamarind water to give it more flavour. Feel free to add baby onions, drumsticks, small eggplants, okra or any vegetable that suits your fancy.

PREP TIME: 15 MIN. | COOKING TIME: 20 MIN. | SERVES: 4–6

250 gm baby onions
2 pods peeled garlic
3 tsp thick tamarind pulp
2 tsp sambar powder
¼ tsp mustard seeds
¼ tsp fenugreek seeds
¼ tsp carom seeds
2 tbsp sesame oil
4 dry red chillies
2 tomatoes
a few curry leaves
a few chopped coriander leaves
salt to taste

Peel the baby onions and set them aside.

Chop the tomatoes finely. Break the red chillies.

Heat the oil and add mustard seeds, fenugreek seeds, carom seeds, dry chillies and curry leaves.

Sauté well, add the onions and fry them till golden brown. Add the garlic flakes.

Add tomatoes, sambar powder and salt.

Then add tamarind pulp and a cup of water.

Cover and cook on low flame for 10 minutes.

When it thickens, remove from fire and garnish with coriander leaves.

TANGY MIXED VEGETABLES

All Tamilian households have their own versions of this dish and this one is from Dad's side of the family in Tanjore. Five or six country vegetables are generally used that give the dish its flavour and colour. The kitchen would brighten up with our lively chatter and the different coloured vegetables would fill the pots as Mom supervised each one of us in cutting the vegetables evenly.

PREP TIME: 30 MIN. | COOKING TIME: 20 MIN. | SERVES: 6–8

100 gm sweet potatoes	Cut all the vegetables 1-inch thick.
100 gm tapioca	Fry the onions, mustard and fenugreek seeds, and curry leaves.
100 gm eggplant	Add the vegetables and pour water.
100 gm sweet pumpkin	Add salt, turmeric, chilli powder and coriander powder.
100 gm white pumpkin	Add coconut milk and cook till the vegetables are cooked.
100 gm potatoes	Add the tamarind pulp and boil for 5–10 minutes.
2 drumsticks	Finally add jaggery.
2 raw mangoes	
2 raw bananas	
2 onions	
1 cup thick coconut milk	
5 cups water	
½ cup thick tamarind pulp	
3 tbsp sesame oil	
1–2 tbsp chilli powder	
2 tbsp coriander powder	
½ tsp turmeric powder	
1 tsp mustard seeds	
1 tsp fenugreek seeds	
1 tbsp jaggery (or as per preference)	
a few curry leaves	
salt to taste	

YAM CURRY

Popular in our home, this recipe uses extra garlic and mustard seeds to give it a spicier flavour.

PREP TIME: 10 MIN. | COOKING TIME: 20 MIN. | SERVES: 4–6

250 gm yam
2 tbsp ginger–garlic paste
3 tbsp tamarind pulp
1 tsp garam masala
1 tsp red chilli powder
¼ tsp turmeric powder
½ tsp mustard seeds
2 onions
3 tomatoes cut
3 green chillies
a few curry leaves
a few fresh coriander leaves
3 tbsp sesame oil
salt to taste

Peel and cut the yam into small pieces and put them to boil. Once they are half done, drain the water, add garam masala, chilli powder, salt and turmeric and mix the masala into the yam well. Heat the oil and add mustard seeds, curry leaves, onions and ginger–garlic paste.
Sauté well, then add tomatoes, green chillies and the yam.
Add tamarind paste and cook on a low flame till tender.
Garnish with fresh coriander.

EGGS

Egg is a superfood, so versatile and fast to cook that it constituted most of our quick-fix meals, simply enhanced by my mother's special touch. She jazzed up the dishes with spicy flavours and the 'hungry us' would come home to a plate of egg cutlets, which would be devoured in seconds. There were days when we didn't feel like eating chicken or meat, but we never said no to egg sambal or egg curry—mom's style!

MOM's EGG CURRY

When I was jotting down this recipe, it brought up vivid memories of curry-soaked idlis and appams, which we would eat with Mom's egg curry—I could almost smell its aroma wafting through my house.

PREP TIME: 30 MIN. | COOKING TIME: 40 MIN. | SERVES: 6

6 eggs	Hardboil the eggs, shell and set aside.
2 tbsp coriander seeds	Cut the onions and slit the green chillies lengthwise.
1 tbsp fenugreek seeds	Grate the coconut and grind it to extract the milk.
½ tsp mustard seeds	Roast the coriander seeds, red chillies and fenugreek seeds and grind them along with the onions.
4 dry red chillies	
6 green chillies	Heat the oil and fry the onion–masala paste, add ginger–garlic paste and fry till the oil separates.
4 onions	
1 tsp turmeric powder	Add the green chillies and fry for 5 more minutes. Then add turmeric and one cup of water.
1 tbsp ginger–garlic paste	
1 fresh coconut	Cover and cook for 15 minutes.
2 sprigs curry leaves	Add the coconut milk and cook on low flame till the curry thickens slightly.
a few coriander leaves	
3 tbsp oil	Add the deshelled boiled eggs and cook for 5 minutes or till you achieve your desired consistency.
salt to taste	

In another pan, heat the oil, add mustard seeds, curry leaves and 2 whole red chillies. Fry till aromatic and add this to the egg curry. Garnish with chopped coriander leaves.

Serve with steamed rice, dosa, appams or idli.

Note:
For extracting coconut milk, check Spices, Stocks and Masalas page 288.

EGG SAMBAL

This dish is a typical Malay way to turn eggs into a hearty, aromatic and delightful meal. You will see why it is one of the family's favourites.

PREP TIME: 10 MIN. | COOKING TIME: 20 MIN. | SERVES: 6

6 eggs	Boil and peel the eggs.
1–2 tbsp red chilli powder	Grind the onions and tomatoes into two separate pastes.
¼ tsp turmeric powder	Roll and tie the lemongrass.
2 onions, ground	Heat the oil and add the onion paste and ginger–garlic paste.
3 tbsp ginger–garlic paste	Sauté the masala till golden brown.
5 tomatoes	Add the lemongrass and tomato paste.
¼ cup oil	Sauté for 5 minutes. Add the chilli powder and turmeric.
2–4 sprigs of lemongrass	Cook till aromatic. Finally cut the eggs lengthwise and place on the masala.
salt to taste	Cook on low flame for 5 minutes. Do not stir.

Serve with steamed rice, rotis or bread.

STUFFED EGG CUTLET

This recipe is a great replacement to the usual cutlets made with meat mince or potatoes. When my friends would holler for me to come out and play with them I would wrap a few of the egg cutlets in serviettes and run off to play cricket in the empty lanes outside (the days when Bangalore roads were a playing field for children and a paradise for all).

PREP TIME: 15 MIN. | COOKING TIME: 20 MIN. | SERVES: 6

6 eggs	Finely chop the onion, green chillies, coriander leaves, ginger and garlic.
4 green chillies	
1-inch ginger piece	Beat one egg.
1 onion	Boil the potatoes and mash them to a smooth consistency.
1 tsp pepper powder	Hardboil the remaining eggs. Put them into cold water, quickly take them out, deshell and slice them into half. Remove the yolks and set them aside.
½ tsp turmeric powder	
6 cloves garlic	
1 packet breadcrumbs	Mix the mashed potatoes with the yolks, salt and pepper powder.
2 potatoes	Fry onions, green chillies, ginger, garlic and turmeric. Add the coriander leaves.
flour	
(seasoned with paprika, salt, pepper and fresh herbs)	Add the potato–yolk mix, stir well and remove from fire.
	Roll the mixture into 12 balls. Stuff each into a half egg white.
1 cup oil	Form into a full egg shape.
a few coriander leaves	Roll each one in the seasoned flour and then dip into the beaten egg.
salt to taste	Finally roll each ball in the breadcrumbs.
	Set aside for 30 minutes.
	Deep-fry till golden brown and serve hot.

EGGS STUFFED WITH COTTAGE CHEESE

The combination of egg yolk and cottage cheese gives this dish that extra filling without making it too heavy to digest.

PREP TIME: 10 MIN. | COOKING TIME: 20 MIN. | SERVES: 6

6 eggs (keep one for breadcrumb mixture)	Boil and deshell 5 eggs, cut them in half lengthwise and take out the yolk.
1 tbsp red chilli powder	Crumble the cottage cheese.
50 gm breadcrumbs	Heat the ghee, add the cottage cheese to it and cook on low flame for a few minutes.
1 tbsp flour	
250 gm cottage cheese	Add milk, garam masala, chilli powder and egg yolks. Add salt.
3 tsp clarified butter (ghee)	Fry for a few minutes and then let the mixture cool.
½ cup milk	Fill the mixture into a boiled egg white, and roll each egg in the flour.
1 tbsp garam masala	
2 cups oil	Make a mixture of 1 beaten egg and the breadcrumbs. Dip the flour-coated egg whites into this mixture and deep fry.
salt to taste	

Serve hot with tomato or chilli sauce.

EGG CURRY

All our friends had a special relationship with my mother and they had no qualms about inviting themselves over to our home to gorge on yummy food, lovingly prepared by her. This dish was one of their favourites.

PREP TIME: 10 MIN. | COOKING TIME: 20 MIN. | SERVES: 6

6 eggs	Boil the eggs, deshell and set them aside.
2 onions	Dry roast the whole spices (cinnamon, cloves), red chillies, coriander seeds, cumin seeds, fennel seeds.
3 tomatoes	
3 cardamoms	Add the poppy seeds and broken cashew nuts and sauté well.
10 peppercorns	Add the grated coconut. Sauté till aromatic and then grind the mixture to a paste. Grind the onions, ginger and garlic as well.
2 tbsp coriander seeds	
1 tbsp fennel seeds	Heat the oil in a deep pan, add the curry leaves and mustard seeds and sauté well, add the onion paste, sauté well and then add the chopped tomatoes.
1 tbsp cumin seeds	
2 tbsp poppy seeds	
1 tsp mustard seeds	Cook till the tomatoes are soft. Add the roasted paste and some water and salt and cook till the curry is thick and the oil separates.
1-inch cinnamon stick	
4 cloves	Add the boiled eggs, cover for a few minutes.
1-inch ginger piece	
1 pod garlic	*Serve with ghee rice or roti.*
½ tsp turmeric powder	
6 dried red chillies	
a few curry leaves	
5 cashew nuts	
½ grated coconut	
2 tbsp oil	
salt to taste	

POULTRY

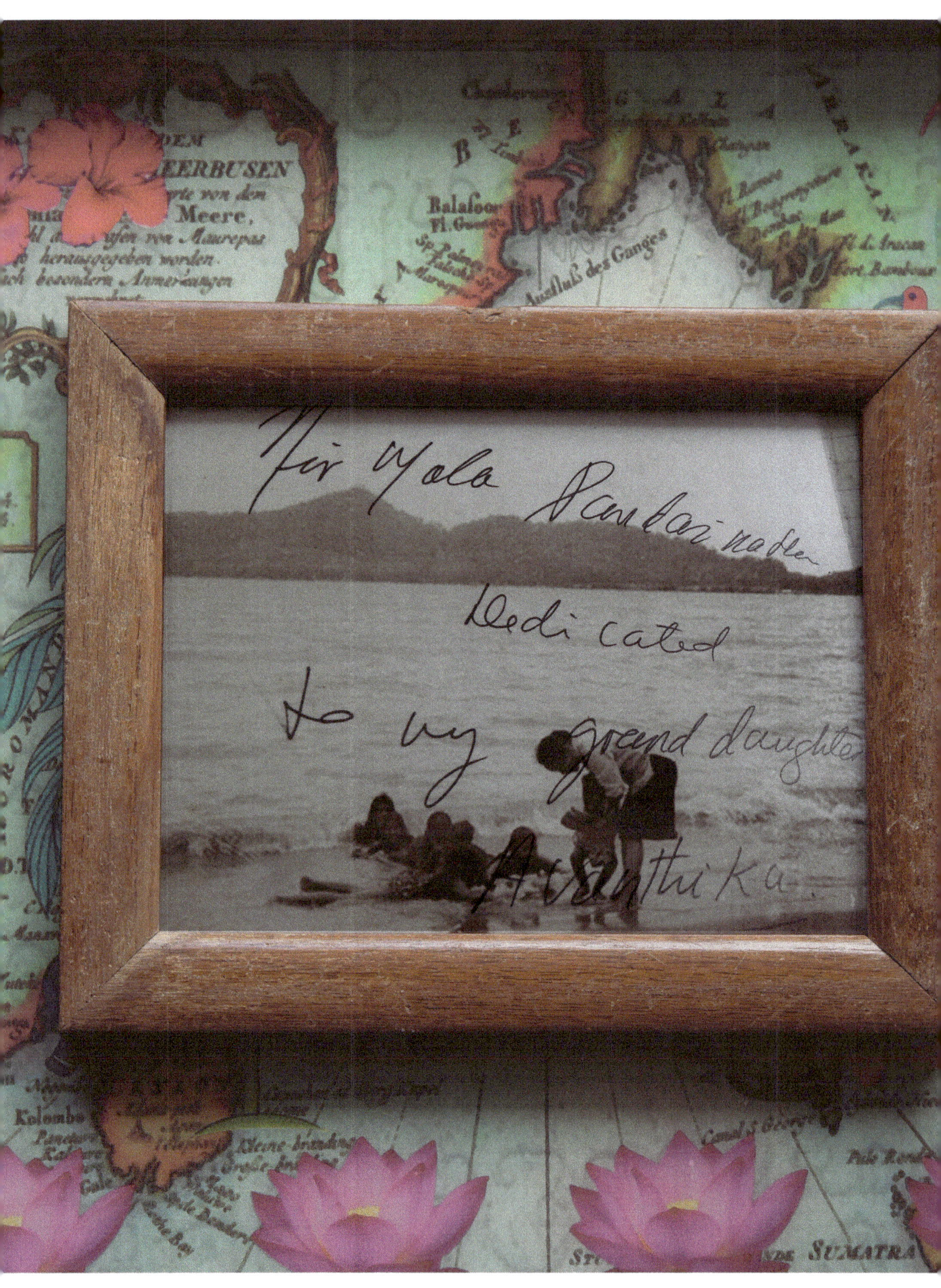

Für Mala Pantai nadu

Dedicated to my granddaughter

Avanthika.

The bond between grandparents and grandchildren is indeed the most cherished one; perhaps it is the wisdom of age and the energy of youth coming together. Our home was no exception and the many special moments between 'Paati' (grandmother) and her grandkids in the kitchen resulted in some great dishes and many delightful memories.

My niece, Avantika, has been a huge fan of many of the recipes mentioned in this chapter. She loved the way my mother's chicken was tender and juicy no matter what she cooked. When she was younger, Avantika would sit on the kitchen countertop, watching her grandmother cooking away and listening to her non-stop chatter about what the menu for the day should be. Mom indulged her by letting her 'help', whereby the grandchild became the executive chef and the grandma the sous chef!

CHICKEN KURMA

Avantika would relish her favourite chicken kurma especially made by her grandma on quite a few of her birthdays. Being Mom's dearest granddaughter, they shared many special grandmother-granddaughter rituals. One of the cutest rituals was at our farmhouse in Madurai where they would go hand in hand and pluck henna leaves off the shrubs, grind them into a paste and apply them in intricate designs on Avantika's palms. That, of course, meant Mom would have to tenderly feed ghee rice with yummy chicken kurma to Avantika later in the day.

PREP TIME: 15 MIN. | COOKING TIME: 60 MIN. | SERVES: 4

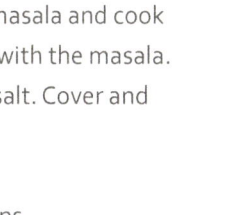

1 kg chicken
3 tomatoes
10 green chillies
1 tsp cumin seeds
1 tsp poppy seeds
½ tsp fennel seeds
2 tbsp coriander seeds
2 cardamoms
2 cloves
1-inch cinnamon stick
1 tbsp peppercorns
2 onions
½ tsp turmeric powder
250 gm potatoes
1-inch ginger piece
1 pod garlic
2 cups water
100 gm cashew nuts
a few curry leaves
a few mint leaves (optional)
a few coriander leaves
3 tbsp sesame oil
1 cup fresh coconut milk
½ a coconut
salt to taste

Skin and cut the chicken into medium-sized pieces.
Scrape the coconut. Cut into small pieces.
Slit the green chillies.
Cut the onions, tomatoes and coriander leaves.
Peel the potatoes and cut them into quarters.
Roast the coconut, poppy seeds, cumin seeds, peppercorn, fennel seeds, coriander seeds, garlic, ginger and cashew nuts, then cool and grind them to a paste.
Heat the oil and fry the chopped onions and cardamoms, cinnamon, cloves, curry leaves and slit green chillies. When slightly brown add the chopped tomatoes. Cook till tender.
Add the chicken pieces and mix them well with the masala and cook for 5 minutes. Add the potatoes and coat well again with the masala.
Add 2 cups of water, stir and then add turmeric and salt. Cover and boil for 10 minutes.
Add the masala paste and add 1 cup coconut milk.
Cook until the chicken is tender and the gravy thickens.
Garnish with finely chopped coriander leaves.

Serve with ghee rice or coconut rice
(recipe given later in the chapter on rice dishes).

MOM's CHICKEN CURRY

'The world's best chicken curry', is how Avantika described the dish and it's on her insistence that I have added this mouth-watering recipe in this book.

PREP TIME: 10 MIN. | COOKING TIME: 40 MIN. | SERVES: 4

1 kg chicken	Clean the chicken and cut into medium-sized pieces.
3 cups coconut milk	Slit the green chillies lengthwise.
2 tbsp ginger–garlic paste	Grind the poppy seeds, musk melon seeds and almonds to a paste.
10 almonds	Heat the oil, sauté the ginger–garlic paste for a few minutes and then add the green chillies.
1 tbsp ghee	
1 tsp garam masala	Add the chicken and fry till golden brown.
10 gm poppy seeds	Add the grounded paste, garam masala, nutmeg, poppy seeds, cardamoms, green chillies and salt.
10 gm musk melon seeds	
¼ tsp nutmeg	Fry for about 10 minutes and then add the coconut milk.
5 cardamoms	Cook on low flame.
6 green chillies	When the gravy is thick add saffron strands.
a few strands saffron	Cook until the chicken is tender.
a few coriander leaves	Garnish with chopped coriander leaves.
salt to taste	

Serve with ghee rice.

TANJORE CHICKEN PEPPER FRY

Dad had a special liking for all dishes cooked in the style of his home town, so naturally this recipe featured at the top of his best food list.

PREP TIME: 10 MIN. | COOKING TIME: 30 MIN. | SERVES: 4

1 kg chicken	Wash and cut the chicken into small pieces.
3 tbsp ginger–garlic paste	Finely chop the onions.
100 gm peppercorns	Dry grind the peppercorns.
¼ cup oil	Break the cinnamon and the dry red chillies into medium-sized pieces.
¼ tsp turmeric powder	Pour the oil in a deep frying pan or kadai and fry the cinnamon, cloves, cardamoms, curry leaves, peeled garlic and onions till golden brown; add the ginger–garlic paste, broken red chillies, salt and turmeric.
10 dry red chillies	
2 onions	
1 pod peeled garlic	Add the chicken and fry for 5–7 minutes and then add half a cup of water; cover and cook on low flame. Keep stirring until it is drier and cooked.
5 cardamoms	
5 cloves	
1-inch cinnamon stick	Add the pepper powder and fry for 5 minutes, remove from the stove.
a few curry leaves	
salt to taste	*Serve with rotis or rice.*

Note:
You can use the same method for mutton pepper fry.
You may also add 2 cups of coconut milk after adding the chicken/mutton, for a different flavour.

CHETTINAD CHICKEN CURRY

The much-loved Chettinad chicken curry would be polished off in no time by us. Other than the fact that Mom loved watching people relish her food, she was equally happy when she could avoid serving them leftovers.

PREP TIME: 20 MIN. | COOKING TIME: 30 MIN. | SERVES: 6–8

1 large chicken
1 large coconut
2 large potatoes

For Seasoning
3 large onions
3 large tomatoes
2-inch cinnamon stick (break into 4)
2 tbsp chilli powder
4 tsp coriander powder
2 tsp turmeric powder
4 tsp ginger–garlic paste
2 tsp fennel seeds
1 lemon-sized tamarind ball
3 tbsp sesame oil
a few curry leaves and coriander leaves
salt to taste

Cut chicken into 14 pieces, wash and rub some salt and turmeric and keep aside.

Soak the tamarind for 10 minutes and extract the pulp.

Grate and grind the coconut to extract 1½ cups of thick milk and grind again to extract 1½ cups of thinner milk. Keep aside.

Wash and finely chop the onions, tomatoes and coriander leaves.

Heat the oil, add the onions, cinnamon, fennel seeds and curry leaves and sauté till golden brown.

Add ginger–garlic paste, chilli powder, turmeric and coriander powder, fry for a few minutes.

Add the tomatoes and stir fry. Then add the chicken pieces, sauté well and add the thinner coconut milk.

Cover and cook for 10 minutes, then add the thick coconut milk, cook until the chicken is tender.

Add potatoes, each chopped into four large pieces. Add the tamarind pulp, simmer for 5 minutes.

Garnish with chopped coriander leaves.

Serve with rice.

CHICKEN IN CASHEW CURRY

Creamy and delicately flavoured, this alternative to the usual hot red curries originated in Kerala. It tastes best with coconut rice, soft fluffy appam, roti and even simple steamed rice. Serve it with a spicy vegetable dish and a tangy pickle and let the party in your mouth begin!

PREP TIME: 20 MIN. | COOKING TIME: 30 MIN. | SERVES: 4–6

1 kg chicken
20 cashew nuts
1 large coconut
3 tbsp oil/ghee

Roast and Grind
2-inch cinnamon stick
5 cloves
5 cardamoms
2-inch ginger piece
20 garlic cloves
2 cups beaten yoghurt
1 tsp fennel seeds
2 tbsp coriander seeds
2 tsp cumin seeds
1 large onion
4–6 green chillies

For Seasoning
2 onions sliced
3 cloves
1-inch cinnamon
juice of 1 lime
3 tbsp ghee/oil
2 bay leaves
a few coriander leaves
a few curry leaves
salt to taste

Wash and cut the chicken into 12 to 14 pieces.

Grind the coconut with water and extract 2 cups of thick milk, then grind again and extract 2 cups of thin milk.

Soak the cashew nuts for 5 to 10 minutes and then grind them.

Mix the beaten yoghurt with the ground masala and rub on to the chicken. Let it marinate for 1 hour.

Heat ghee/oil in a cast-iron pot or any other heavy pan, season and sauté for a few minutes.

Add the chicken pieces to the masala, sauté for a few minutes, add some salt.

After about 10 minutes add the thin coconut milk, reduce the heat and simmer until the chicken is cooked.

Add the thick coconut milk and simmer for 10 minutes.

Remove from heat, add the lime juice.

Garnish with chopped coriander leaves.

Serve with coconut rice or roti.

SINGAPORE AYAM PANGGANG CHICKEN

Originating from Manado, the capital city of Northern Sulawesi, Indonesia, this grilled chicken has been a local delight in Singapore for many years. An adventurous eater, Mom preferred eating in smaller, family-owned establishments frequented by the locals as opposed to the more touristy eateries. 'It's where you get the most authentic food' is what she always said when anyone tried steering her elsewhere. Over the years, my sister and I seem to be following in her footsteps; you know it's true when they say 'Moms know best'. This tangy chicken dish can be added to your barbecue list.

PREP TIME: 10 MIN. | MARINATION TIME: 3 HRS. | COOKING TIME: 60 MIN. | SERVES: 5

- 5 chicken legs or medium-sized chicken breasts
- 2 onions
- 1 cup coconut cream/milk
- 2 lemon leaves
- 2 fresh turmeric leaves
- 2 small-sized balls tamarind
- 2 tsp ginger paste
- 2 tsp garlic paste
- 2 tbsp chilli paste
- 2 tsp fresh turmeric powder
- 4 tbsp pine nuts (optional)
- 2 sprigs lemongrass
- 400 ml chicken stock
- 2 tbsp oil
- salt and pepper to taste

Grind the onions, ginger, garlic, fresh turmeric and pine nuts into a paste. Add pepper and salt.

Add the chilli paste, mix it with the chicken and marinate for 3 hours in the fridge.

Grill the marinated chicken until cooked evenly brown.

Heat a wok and add the remaining marinated paste and all other ingredients except the coconut cream and simmer for 15 minutes.

Add chicken stock, salt and pepper, coconut cream and simmer for 30 minutes more.

When thick, pour over the grilled chicken.

Serve it with roti jala (recipe on the next page).

ROTI JALA

These beautiful cup-shaped rotis delicately patterned held my fascination ever since I can remember and Mom would cook them on all my special occasions—birthdays, festivals and other celebration days—for me to feel extra special. The roti jala, unique and flavourful, made me really warm and fuzzy inside.

COOKING TIME: 20 MIN. | SERVES: 2

1 cup (150 gm) all-purpose flour
¼ tsp ground turmeric powder
¼ tsp salt
1 egg beaten
¾ cup (180 ml) coconut milk mixed with ¾ cup water
oil to grease the pan
pandan leaves tied into a knot (used for brushing)
jala mould
(roti jala mould is a cup with 5 to 6 nozzles to make tender, delicate, lacy crepes in Malaysia)

Sift the flour and turmeric into a large bowl. Add salt. Stir in the beaten egg and coconut milk until a smooth batter forms.
Strain batter to remove any lumps.
Brush oil on to a heated pan using the pandan leaves.
Pour a little batter into the roti jala mould until about half full. Move the cup over the pan in a circular motion to form a lacy pattern.
Cook until set. Takes only about 2 minutes.
Slide crepe out of the pan on to a plate. Repeat until batter is finished. When cool enough fold both sides of the crepe and roll to form a neat package.

Serve with Singapore Ayam Panggang Chicken or chicken in cashew curry.

CHICKEN IN CURRY LEAVES AND NUTS

A tangy fried chicken with peanut powder and curry leaves was on my request list very often and Mom always surprised me by cooking it in a jiffy.

PREP TIME: 10 MIN. | COOKING TIME: 25 MIN. | SERVES: 2

500 gm chicken
1 lemon
½ tsp turmeric powder
1 tbsp chilli powder
2 tsp coriander powder
2 onions
5 green chillies
50 gm peanuts
15 garlic flakes
2 tbsp oil
1-inch ginger piece chopped finely
a few curry leaves
a few coriander leaves
salt to taste

Wash, clean and cut the chicken into small pieces, rub them with salt and turmeric powder, chilli powder, coriander powder and ½ tsp oil and keep aside.
Fry the peanuts and powder them.
Heat the oil, rub the peanut powder on the chicken, mix well and fry till golden brown and keep aside.

You could also shallow fry the chicken if you wish.
Fry the green chillies, onions, curry leaves, chopped ginger and garlic.
Add the fried chicken to the mix and stir well.
Garnish with coriander leaves.

LANKAN CHICKEN CURRY

Not just Mom but our whole family and a few of our dearest friends have a deep fondness for this island country of immense beauty, rich culture and great warmth. The Lankan chicken curry is the perfect example of the country's delectable cuisine.

PREP TIME: 20 MIN. | COOKING TIME: 30 MIN. | SERVES: 4

1 kg chicken
1-inch ginger shredded
2 cloves garlic crushed
2 cardamoms crushed
2 cloves crushed
15 shallots diced
2 fresh green chillies sliced
1 tsp chilli powder
½ tsp cinnamon powder
2 tsp pepper powder
3 tbsp curry powder
¼ tsp turmeric powder
2 tbsp tamarind pulp
3 tbsp oil
1-inch cinnamon stick
2 long stems lemongrass
a few curry leaves
¼ tsp fenugreek seeds
2 cups thick coconut milk
½ tbsp lime juice
salt to taste

Clean and cut the chicken into medium-sized pieces.

Add cardamoms, cloves, garlic, chillies, ginger, pepper powder, tamarind water, curry powder, turmeric powder, salt, cinnamon powder, chilli powder in a bowl. Mix well and rub the mix on to the chicken pieces and marinate for 1 hr.

Heat oil in a pan, add the cinnamon stick, lemongrass, curry leaves, fenugreek seeds and chopped shallots. Fry for a few minutes.

Add the chicken marinade and stir fry for 3 minutes.

Pour coconut milk and mix well.

Cook over low flame for 40 minutes till the chicken is tender.

Sprinkle over with lime juice.

Serve hot with rice.

Good food is very often,
even most often, simple food.
—Anthony Bourdain

MEATS

Mom loved everything to do with meat—shopping for it, prepping it, cooking it and most of all experimenting with it, and she had a plethora of recipes to prove it.

Shopping for meat and vegetables, old Bangaloreans will agree, had to be at the crowded, noisy and busy Russel Market. From fresh flowers at the entrance to green vegetables, fish and meat, every possible knick-knack was to be found at Bangalore's oldest market. Bangaloreans from the 1980s and earlier remember parking luxuriously outside the famous Russel Market before stepping into the cauldron of exciting smells and colours.

That was our market morning ritual holding on to Mom's hands tightly; skipping past candies, dried fruits and spices; steering through the narrow lanes in search of the freshest cuts of meat. Mom's sharp sense of smell would get a whiff of the best and the freshest despite the chaos. We would watch in amazement as she oscillated from bantering with the local vendors to gently bargaining and before we knew it we were whisked off to the next stage of shopping with mutton and mince parcelled neatly into our baskets—precious goodies purchased at a steal.

Many Bangalorean foodies will swear by this place for its cold cuts and pork—the Bangalore Ham Shop on M.G. Road in existence since the 1930s. Mom's association with it goes way back to her boarding school days when she would accompany the cook to this iconic charcuterie.

The recipes in this chapter consist of some of her favourites and a few of ours.

MUTTON PEPPER FRY

We relished this dish for its spicy kick and had the thickened gravy with piping hot rotis, dal and rice. When the zest of spicy pepper is tempered down with rich coconut milk, the result is simply divine.

PREP TIME: 10 MIN. | COOKING TIME: 40 MIN. | SERVES: 6–8

1 kg boneless mutton	Wash and cut the mutton into medium-sized chunks and finely chop the onions.
2 large onions	
1-inch cinnamon stick	Heat the oil in a pan and sauté the onions and the ginger–garlic paste in it.
2 tbsp chilli powder	
2 tbsp pepper powder	Add the cinnamon, mutton, chillies, turmeric powder and salt.
1 cup coconut milk (or coconut flakes)	Sauté for 15 minutes and then add the coconut milk or coconut flakes. Lower the flame.
2 tbsp ginger–garlic paste	Cook till the mutton is three-fourths done, then add the curry leaves and cook till tender and dry.
½ tsp turmeric powder	
¼ cup oil	Finally add the pepper and mix well on low flame.
a few curry leaves	Garnish with coriander leaves.
salt to taste	
a few coriander leaves	

LAMB CHOPS

While all of us were forbidden to eat by the plunge pool in our farmhouse when we were kids, the grandkids were given a special pass by Mom. She would send out a steaming plate of lamb chops for her darling grandchildren. The little rascals knew just how to win her over and made it a point to describe the delight of digging into the warm and spicy fry when they were ravenous from frolicking around in the pool.

When you really want to prepare a feast for someone, do include these chops. You can't go wrong and there won't be any leftovers. Guests who had eaten them before would always request for them to be added to the menu.

PREP TIME: 10 MIN. | MARINATION TIME: 30 MIN. | COOKING TIME: 30 MIN. | SERVES: 6–8

Ingredients	Method
1 kg lamb chops	Wash the lamb chops and marinate them with pepper, chilli powder, turmeric powder, ginger–garlic paste and a little salt for 30 minutes.
3 eggs	
2 tbsp ginger–garlic paste	Pressure cook with 3–5 cups of water for about 3 whistles.
2 cups all-purpose flour	Whisk the eggs and salt in a bowl.
2 tbsp pepper powder	Heat the oil in a deep frying pan.
2 tbsp coriander powder	Dip each lamb chop into egg and then roll over the flour; make sure they are well coated.
3 tbsp chilli powder	
½ tsp turmeric powder	Fry the chops till golden brown and serve hot.
2 cups oil	
salt to taste	

MUTTON WITH GONGURA LEAVES

Gongura leaves or sorrel leaves are known to be an excellent source of folate, B6, zinc, calcium, vitamins C and A and antioxidants. They are intrinsic to Telugu cuisine. The mutton cooked with these leaves is packed with a tangy punch and sure to bring variety to your table. The key to this dish is to balance the ingredients to get the right amount of tanginess from the leaves.

PREP TIME: 20 MIN. | COOKING TIME: 40 MIN. | SERVES: 6–8

1 kg mutton (pressure-cooked)
2 cups fresh red gongura/sorrel leaves
1 cup thick coconut milk
5–6 green chillies
1 tsp poppy seeds
½ tsp fennel seeds
½ tsp cumin seeds
4–5 cardamoms
4 medium-sized finely chopped onions
1 tbsp coriander powder
½ tsp clove powder
½ tsp cinnamon powder
1 tbsp chilli powder
3 tbsp curry powder
¼ tsp turmeric powder
2 tbsp ginger–garlic paste
¼ cup oil
2 sprigs curry leaves
salt to taste

Heat in a pot, add onions, cardamoms, cloves, slit green chillies and curry leaves. Fry till the onions are brown.

Grind the poppy seeds, cumin seeds and fennel seeds, roast them and add to the mix made in step 1. Add the coriander powder and chilli powder. Keep aside.

Boil the gongura leaves after cleaning them and grind them to a fine paste. Add this paste to the masala with 4 cups of water and boil for 10 minutes.

Add pressure-cooked mutton and salt. Cook for 20 minutes.

Add the coconut milk and boil for 10 minutes till the gravy is thick.

Serve with rice.

MINCED MUTTON CUTLETS

These make a great appetiser which my mother usually served with a mint and garlic chutney or a simple creamy garlic dip for a zingier bite.

COOKING TIME: 30 MIN. | SERVES: 6–8

½ kg minced mutton
2 onions
1 tsp turmeric powder
4 green chillies
1 tsp coriander powder
2 bread slices
2 tsp ginger–garlic paste
1 egg
2 cups water
4 cups breadcrumbs
1 sprig coriander leaves
3 cups oil
salt to taste

Wash the mince and squeeze it dry.
Soak the bread slices in water and squeeze out the water.
Beat the egg.
Finely chop the onions, green chillies, coriander leaves.
Mix the onions, green chillies, ginger–garlic paste, coriander leaves, salt, turmeric powder, bread slices, and beaten egg into the mince.
Mix well and divide into 10 to 12 portions.
Shape into flat round cutlets and roll each one in breadcrumbs.
Heat the oil and fry the cutlets on a low flame till golden brown.

Note:
Use the same method for chicken mince, minced squid/prawns, crabs or semi-cooked fish.

KARI KEEMA KEMBING
(minced lamb in coconut sauce)

Southeast Asian flavours found special favour with Mom and ever so often the Kari Kembing with its easy to cook and subtle flavours made its way to our table.

COOKING TIME: 30 MIN. | SERVES: 4

½ kg mutton mince
4 tbsp red chilli paste
5 cinnamon sticks
½ kg onions
4 tbsp ginger–garlic paste
5 cloves
½ kg tomatoes
2 tbsp sugar
5 cardamoms
salt to taste
1 cup coconut milk
2 tsp aniseed powder
a few coriander leaves
¼ cup oil for frying

Wash and drain the mince well. Mince onions and puree the tomatoes.
Heat oil in a pan and fry the onions till transparent. Add the ginger–garlic paste and the whole spices. Fry till golden brown.
Add the tomato puree and lamb. Cook till oil floats on the top.
Then add the chilli paste, salt and sugar. Sauté well and add the coconut milk.
Cover and cook till done.

Serve with steamed rice and rotis.

MUTTON BRAIN SEEKH

A mutton brain smeared with a paste of chillies, spices and coconut and simply baked is such an easy but yummy way of preparing a delicacy, relished by many a meat lover.

COOKING TIME: 25 MIN. | BAKING TIME: 20 MIN. | SERVES: 4

1 brain	Wash and clean the brain, boil it with a pinch of turmeric and salt till tender.
3 eggs	
6 green chillies	Grind the coriander, cumin, green chillies, lime juice, salt and coconut to a paste. Beat the eggs. Cut the potatoes into any shape and crisp-fry them.
½ tsp cumin seeds	
2 tsp turmeric powder	
1 small piece of coconut	Apply the ground paste to the cooked brain and place it on a baking tray.
1 lemon	
3 potatoes	Pour the beaten eggs over the brain and sprinkle salt and pepper, and bake for about 20 minutes in the oven.
1 tsp pepper powder	
4 tbsp oil	Garnish with lettuce leaves and fried potatoes.
1 bunch coriander leaves	
a few lettuce leaves	Note:
salt to taste	Ensure the mutton brain is thoroughly washed and cleaned by the butcher.

PEPPER MASALA MUTTON CHOPS

I can't remember a single time when mutton chops in pepper masala came out tasting less than perfect. Dad and my nephew Anush are testimony to that since we wouldn't hear a peep from them until every last morsel on their plates had been devoured.

PREP TIME: 10 MIN. | COOKING TIME: 40 MIN. | SERVES: 6–8

1 kg mutton chops
2 onions
4 tomatoes
1 tsp garam masala
¼ cup oil
1 cup coconut milk
½ tsp turmeric powder
2 tbsp black pepper powder
2 tbsp chilli powder
1 tbsp coriander powder
1 tbsp ginger–garlic paste
a few curry leaves
a few coriander leaves
salt to taste

Wash and rub a little pepper powder, chilli powder, turmeric powder, ginger–garlic paste and a little salt into the mutton and set aside for 30 minutes.

Pressure cook the mutton to 3 whistles with 1 cup of water.

Finely chop the onions and tomatoes.

Heat the oil and fry the onions, sauté for a few minutes and then add the remaining ginger–garlic paste.

Sauté and add the chopped tomatoes, chilli powder, coriander powder and garam masala.

Cook for 5 minutes, add the coconut milk and the chops.

Cook till tender and when the masala is dry add the pepper powder and the curry leaves.

Serve hot with rice or rotis or iddiappams.

IRISH STEW

Light and flavourful, we often devoured the stew by dipping hot garlic bread into it, but it could also be served with appams and rice flour rotis. This wholesome dish was from Mom's days in England. If you prefer to make fresh chicken stock, make sure that you let the stock simmer on a low flame so that it turns out to be clear instead of murky.

PREP TIME: 20 MIN. | COOKING TIME: 30 MIN. | SERVES: 6

500 gm lamb with bones or lamb shoulder
6 slices or 100 gm smoked streaky sliced bacon
2 potatoes cut into chunks
2 carrots pieces of 2-inches
15–20 French beans (cut into 1-inch pieces)
1 tbsp dried rosemary
2 sprigs fresh rosemary
2 bay leaves
small bunch thyme
knob of butter
3 spring onions finely chopped
1 tbsp crushed pepper
1½ tbsp all-purpose flour
3 tbsp milk
2 cups chicken or lamb stock
2 cups water
salt to taste

Heat a pan and fry the bacon crisp and place aside.
Use the same pan and fry the potatoes and spring onions.
Add the lamb and fry for 5–7 minutes then add all the vegetables, rosemary, pepper, salt, crushed pieces of bacon, bay leaves, salt, lamb stock, water, and fresh rosemary sprigs.
Cover and cook until the lamb is well cooked.
Mix the all-purpose flour in the milk, add it to the stew.
Slow cook till the lamb is completely well done.

For the Lamb Stock
Bones from the lamb
1 onion cut in half
2 carrots chopped into 3 pieces
2 celery stalks chopped into 3 pieces
6–8 parsley sprigs
10 peppercorns
8–9 cups water
salt to taste

Place the lamb bones and other pieces in a pot.
Add all other ingredients and the salt.
Bring to a boil and let it simmer for 2 hours.
Remove large bones and pieces and strain.
Cool and store in an airtight container in the fridge (can keep for 5–6 days) or freeze (can keep for 2 months).

TROTTER STEW

*No non-vegetarian cooking would be complete without having tried
the paaya—a classic dish full of aromatic spices.
This hearty meal is recommended for anyone who is recuperating from illness or debility.*

PREP TIME: 15 MIN. | MARINATION TIME: 2 HRS. | COOKING TIME: 15 MIN. | SERVES: 4–6

6 trotters	Wash and clean the trotters.
2 onions	Chop onions, tomatoes and garlic, and shred the ginger.
4–6 garlic pods	Cut all the vegetables to 1-inch size. Slit the chillies.
2-inch ginger piece	Heat oil, add and sauté well the onions, green chillies, ginger, garlic, cinnamon stick and the trotters. Add 6 cups of water, boil, and simmer for 3 hours.
4 green chillies	
6 cups water	
4 tomatoes	Then add the tomatoes, vegetables and the remaining masalas.
6 French beans	Cook on slow flame till tender.
2 carrots	
2 potatoes	
1 tbsp pepper powder	
1 tbsp garam masala	
1-inch cinnamon stick	
1 tbsp cumin seeds	
2 cloves	
oil for cooking	
a few mint leaves	
salt to taste	

MINCED MEATBALL CURRY

It was his twinkling eyes, rubbing his hands with glee and sheer delight on Dad's face when Mom brought this dish to the table that drove her to make it whenever he was around. The frying and simmering of meatballs in Indian spices makes this dish an absolute must-try for meat lovers.

PREP TIME: 40 MIN. | COOKING TIME: 60 MIN. | SERVES: 6–8

500 gm minced mutton
5–6 green chillies
500 gm tomatoes
500 gm onions
500 gm potatoes
250 gm fresh green peas
1 tbsp chilli powder
2 tbsp coriander powder
½ tsp turmeric powder
1 tsp garam masala
4 cloves
4 green cardamoms
3 black cardamoms
1-inch cinnamon stick
½ bunch coriander leaves
½ bunch mint leaves
2 tbsp ginger–garlic paste
5 garlic flakes
2 cups coconut milk
a few curry leaves
3 tbsp oil
salt to taste

Wash the mince and make sure all the water is drained out.

Chop the onions, green chillies and tomatoes finely.

Cut the potatoes into quarters, shell the green peas, wash and set aside.

Grind the mince in a wet grinder and set aside.

Fry 3 chopped onions, add the chopped garlic, mix some chopped coriander, mint leaves, salt, ½ tsp garam masala powder and the green chillies. Add the mince and mix well.

Make lime-sized balls.

In a small wok, heat the oil and fry the onions, ginger–garlic paste, sauté well, then add the whole spices.

Add the tomatoes, cook for 5 minutes, then add all the powdered masala and salt and cook for about 5 minutes or till the oil separates.

Add 1 cup of coconut milk and bring it to a boil. Add meatballs and green peas and potatoes, simmer and cook on a low flame for about 25 minutes.

Check and see if the green peas and meatballs are cooked.

Add the second cup of coconut milk, simmer and cook for 10 minutes. Garnish with curry leaves and coriander leaves.

Serve hot with steamed rice or roti.

MUTTON KURMA

This dish was cooked often at our home and eaten with ghee rice, or coconut rice, or dosas, or idlis or rotis. Mom made a vegetarian version for my brother by using soya chunks and mushrooms. Whatever the version, every last morsel was devoured and relished with gusto by all of us.

PREP TIME: 20 MIN. | COOKING TIME: 60 MIN. | SERVES: 4–6

1 kg mutton	Scrape the ½ coconut. Slit the green chillies.
3 tomatoes	Cut the onions, tomatoes and coriander leaves and peel and quarter the potatoes.
5–8 green chillies	
2 green cardamoms	Dry roast the chopped coconut pieces, poppy seeds, cumin seeds, peppercorns, fennel seeds, coriander seeds, chopped garlic and ginger and cashew nuts. Cool and grind these into a paste.
2 onions	
250 gm potatoes	
1 tsp cumin seeds	Heat the oil and fry the onions and cardamoms, cinnamon, cloves, curry leaves and slit green chillies. When slightly brown, add the tomatoes and cook till tender.
1 tsp poppy seeds	
½ tsp fennel seeds	
2 tbsp coriander seeds	Add chopped mutton pieces and stir well. Add the potatoes and stir well.
10 peppercorns	
1 pod garlic	Add 2 cups of water, stir and add turmeric powder and salt. Cover and boil for 10 minutes.
½ tsp turmeric	
2 cloves	Add the dry roast masala, stir, then add 2 cups of coconut milk.
100 gm cashew nuts	Cook for 15 minutes or until the meat is cooked. Gravy should be thick.
2 cups water	
1-inch cinnamon stick	
1-inch ginger piece	Garnish with finely chopped coriander leaves.
a few curry leaves	
a few coriander leaves	*Serve with ghee rice or coconut rice.*
a few mint leaves	
3 tbsp oil	
½ coconut	
2 cups coconut milk	
salt to taste	

TRADITIONAL SOUTH INDIAN MUTTON CURRY

This delicious, melt-in-the-mouth mutton curry was often our Sunday lunch special. It is traditional, spicy and earthy. It pairs perfectly with coconut rice and onion salad with fried or roasted papads as accompaniments.

PREP TIME: 15 MIN. | MARINATION TIME: 60 MIN. | COOKING TIME: 45 MIN. | SERVES: 6–8

1 kg mutton	Wash and cut the mutton into medium-sized pieces. Mix turmeric powder, ginger–garlic paste and lime juice with the mutton, marinate for 1 hour.
2 tbsp coriander seeds	
1 tbsp fenugreek seeds	
½ tsp mustard seeds	Cut the onions and slit the green chillies.
½ tsp poppy seeds	Grate the coconut and grind to extract milk.
4 onions	Roast the coriander seeds, red chillies and fenugreek seeds and grind them along with the onions.
10 dry red chillies	
8 green chillies	Heat the oil and fry the onion masala paste till the oil separates.
1 coconut scraped (or 1 cup coconut milk)	Add the green chillies and the mutton. Fry for 5 minutes, add one cup of water, cover and cook until three-fourths done.
1 tsp turmeric powder	Add the coconut milk and cook till the mutton is tender.
2 sprigs curry leaves	In another pan heat the oil, add mustard seeds and curry leaves, 2 whole red chillies, and fry till aromatic and add this to the mutton curry.
1 tbsp ginger–garlic paste	
1 tbsp lemon juice	
oil	Garnish with chopped coriander leaves.
a few coriander leaves	
salt to taste	*Serve with steamed rice.*

MUTTON DALCHA

This famous Hyderabadi meat curry is the marrying of a wholesome Bengal gram dal with mutton so you can taste the best of both worlds. Rumour has it that the kitchens of the Nizam of Hyderabad perfected this dish. While the mutton and Bengal gram are the heroes of this dish, the star ingredient is really the tamarind water, which adds the delicate tangy flavour. Also, the mutton must be cooked on low flame so that it turns tender and melts in the mouth just perfectly.

PREP TIME: 20 MIN. | COOKING TIME: 45 MIN. | SERVES: 8

1 kg mutton 500 gm onions 250 gm tomatoes 2 tbsp ginger–garlic paste 1 tsp mustard seeds 250 gm Bengal gram 15 curry leaves ¼ ml coconut milk 1 tbsp turmeric powder 1 tbsp coriander powder 3 tbsp chilli powder 8 dry red chillies 2 green cardamoms 1-inch cinnamon stick chopped coriander leaves 2 medium-sized onions ¼ ml tamarind water ½ bottle gourd 2 drumsticks 3 tbsp oil salt to taste	Wash and clean the mutton pieces and pressure cook these with ginger–garlic paste, salt and turmeric powder. Heat the oil, fry the sliced onions till brown, add cardamoms, cinnamon stick, cloves, ginger–garlic paste, chilli powder, turmeric powder, coriander powder and chopped tomatoes. Fry for 10 minutes and then add the boiled mutton and dal. Pressure cook to 4 whistles. Once cooked add the bottle gourd and drumsticks. Add fresh coconut milk, tamarind juice and boil until the vegetables are cooked. Temper with mustard seeds and curry leaves. *Serve hot with steamed rice or bread.*

BRAIN OMELETTE

My grandmother's brain curry and mutton trotters were famous but it was this dish that stood out among the many accompaniments that Mom cooked. She learnt from our grandmother and Mom always insisted that it be served straight from the pan on to the plate.

PREP TIME: 20 MIN. | COOKING TIME: 45 MIN. | SERVES: 4

1 brain (lamb or goat)
3 eggs
1 large onion
3 tomatoes
2 tsp pepper powder
½ tsp turmeric powder
5 green chillies
a few coriander leaves
2 tbsp oil
salt to taste

Clean the brain, beat the eggs with salt and pepper, add the brain to the eggs and beat well.

To the brain mixture, add the chopped onions, green chillies, tomato and coriander leaves. Put the mixture in oil.

Turn over after a few minutes, cook till both sides are golden brown.

Serve with bread or roti.

Note:
Ensure the mutton brain is thoroughly washed and cleaned by the butcher.

MUTTON STEW

This recipe evolved with Mom experimenting with various herbs and flavours till she finally settled on the ones mentioned below. The apple juice adds a certain sweet flavour to the dish, making it unique as compared to other mutton stews.

PREP TIME: 15 MIN. | COOKING TIME: 2 HRS. | SERVES: 4–6

500 gm boneless mutton
3 tbsp all-purpose flour
1 cup apple juice
250 gm turnips
250 gm carrots
1 tsp marjoram
½ tsp dried thyme
1 tbsp parsley
1 tsp pepper
1 tsp cumin powder
1 tsp coriander powder
500 gm onions
1 kg potatoes
2 tsp butter
1 cup water
1 tbsp oil
salt to taste

Wash and clean the mutton. Slice the onions.

Peel and dice the turnips and carrots.

Boil the potatoes and mash with a little milk, salt and pepper.

Mix 1 tbsp of flour, salt and pepper with the mutton pieces, a few at a time, so that all the pieces are coated well.

In a large saucepan heat the oil and fry the mutton pieces till they are brown.

Add the sliced onions and 1 cup of apple juice, cover and simmer for 1 ½ hours or until the meat is tender (or pressure cook till the meat is tender).

Add the turnip and carrot pieces, 1 cup of water, parsley, salt, marjoram and thyme.

Simmer for about 30 minutes until vegetables are tender.

Blend water and 2 tbsp flour, stir into the mixture, cook and stir till it thickens and bubbles.

Pour into a serving dish, spoon some mashed potatoes around the edge.

Add more chopped chillies or even a pinch of cumin and coriander for the extra kick.

Serve with bread rolls and butter.

FRIED MEATBALLS
(kolla urandai)

These crisp and tender fried meatballs make delightful starters and they always brought out the childlike side of my dad who would be ready to compete with any of us on how many pieces we could devour. In short these entrees are so good you'll need to make a good many to go around.

COOKING TIME: 40 MIN. | SERVES: 4–6

500 gm minced mutton
¼ tsp turmeric powder
½ cup roasted Bengal gram dal
1 bunch coriander leaves
4 shallots
½ coconut grated
5–6 green chillies
1 egg
oil for frying
salt to taste

To Grind
2-inch ginger piece
1 pod garlic
1 tbsp cumin seeds
1-inch cinnamon stick
4 cloves

Wash the mince and make sure all the water is drained out.

Grind ginger, garlic, cinnamon, cloves and cumin seeds to a smooth paste. Add turmeric and mix well.

Add the ground paste to the mince and cook for 10 minutes till all the water has dried out.

Cool and grind the mixture to a coarse paste.

Grind the coconut separately to a paste with very little water.

Chop the onions, green chillies and coriander leaves.

Powder the fried gram dal.

Add the onions, coconut paste, green chillies, coriander leaves, dal, eggs and salt to the ground meat.

Knead the mixture well and make small balls.

Heat the oil in a deep pan and fry till golden brown.

Serve with dal and rice. Pan fry for a healthier version.

LIVER FRY

Classic way to savour liver is to fry it with pepper and curry leaves. Liver fry is a great source of iron, vitamin B, vitamin C and potassium. This recipe is deliciously peppery and tangy, a must-try.

PREP TIME: 15 MIN. | MARINATION TIME: 2 HRS. | COOKING TIME: 15 MIN. | SERVES: 4–6

500 gm mutton liver
2 tbsp pepper
2 tsp coriander powder
2 tomatoes or 1 tsp vinegar
1½-inch cinnamon stick
5 cloves
5 green cardamoms
3–4 fresh green chillies
1 tbsp ginger paste
1 tbsp garlic paste
½ tsp turmeric powder
3–4 tbsp vinegar
1 cup shallots or 2 onions
a few curry leaves
a few coriander leaves
a few mint leaves
oil for frying
salt to taste

Wash and clean the liver, cut it into small pieces and add turmeric and salt and marinate for 2 hours.

Cut the onions and curry leaves and fry till light brown. Add the tomatoes or vinegar and fry.

Grind cinnamon sticks, cloves, cardamoms, green chillies, coriander leaves, mint leaves, ginger–garlic paste, pepper powder, coriander powder and cloves.

Add the paste to the fried onions and curry leaves. Add the marinated liver. Fry it with the masala for a minute or two. Add salt, a little water and cook.

Cook till dry, add curry leaves and garnish with coriander leaves.

Notes:
Turmeric and salt are added to the liver to quicken the marination process.
Cook liver on slow flame for 10-15 minutes.
You can add small pieces of potatoes if needed.

BONELESS LAMB FRY

Dad knew this dish was Avantika's favourite and so he would pick the choicest pieces off her plate and put them on his to tease her. A ruffled Avantika would fight with Dad, who would sit nonchalantly and wolf down the mutton fry merrily. Amidst the entire commotion Mom would come storming out of the kitchen and have Dad sheepishly restore those precious pieces of lamb fry on to Avantika's plate. What can I say—an amazing mutton fry with a possessive fan!

PREP TIME: 10 MIN. | MARINATION TIME: 30 MIN. | COOKING TIME: 40 MIN. | SERVES: 4–6

500 gm boneless lamb
1 pod garlic
1 piece ginger
4 cloves
1 large onion
1 tomato
2 tsp aniseed
1½ tsp poppy seeds
½ tsp turmeric powder
1 tbsp chilli powder
2 tbsp grated coconut
3 green cardamoms
3 cinnamon sticks of 1 inch size
a few peppercorns and curry leaves
2 tbsp coriander seeds
a few coriander leaves
3 tbsp oil
salt to taste

Grind all the ingredients together (except onion and tomato) to a fine paste.

Apply it to the mutton pieces and set aside for half an hour.

Cut the onion finely. Heat the oil and add the chopped onion and fry till golden brown.

Add the mutton pieces and sliced tomato and fry till the oil separates.

Add enough water for the lamb to cook till there is no gravy.

Add the curry leaves.

Garnish with cut coriander leaves.

Serve hot with roti, paratha or rice.

SEAFOOD

The sea held the dearest spot in Mom's heart as almost all of her childhood days were spent on the beaches of Singapore. The flock of siblings would swim, frolic and use tiny nets to catch mussels, crabs and handfuls of shells.

Naturally Mom would take us many times during our summer vacations to our grandparents' home town, Rameswaram—a tiny island off the South Indian peninsula with glorious virgin beaches and the bluest seas compelling us to be beach bums. In the mornings, we lolled on soft sands, created our own waves in the water and squealed when Mom would show us how to catch tiny crabs with our fingers. For lunch, we would walk home through coconut groves and then feast on the catch of the day served with string hoppers. This was how a few of our summers were spent, satiated on seafood, surf and sun.

But it was the early morning trips to the beach when fishermen would bring in their trawlers laden with fresh catch that we really looked forward to. There were times when, for a little extra, the fishermen would let us go out to sea in their trawlers filled with bright blue nets for a short trip. These are memories of a childhood spoilt thoroughly by the goodness of the sea and the simplicity of life. We would hop aboard with Ma in one of the trawlers and watch her pick and choose our lunch from their bounty.

Mom's repertoire of seafood recipes consisted of family secrets that were handed down over generations. But her inherent love for the sea and its bounties coupled with her talent at conjuring up all sorts of fish, prawn and crab delights ensured that we ate a variety of seafood. I highly recommend the stuffed crabs, my mom's fish curry in coconut milk, and fish sambal.

FISH CURRY

A spicy fish curry with thick gravy delicately cooked in a bunch of fragrant spices, it's fabulous to have for breakfast with idiyappam/string hoppers. The fish soaks in the gravy and it's simply divine.

PREP TIME: 15 MIN. | COOKING TIME: 25 MIN. | SERVES: 6–8

1 kg king or seer fish	Wash and clean the fish and cut into slices. Rub with salt, lime juice and turmeric. Keep aside.
250 gm shallots	Peel the shallots and cut the large onions finely.
4–6 tsp red chilli powder	Slit the green chillies. Cut the tomatoes. Fry the fenugreek seeds and pound finely.
4 tsp coriander powder	
1 tsp pepper powder	Pour the oil in a deep vessel and fry the chopped big onions. Then add the whole small onions and add mustard seeds.
1 tsp turmeric powder	
1 tsp fenugreek seeds	Stir well, then add the tomatoes, green chillies and curry leaves.
1 tsp mustard seeds	Stir well and add 1 cup water, chilli powder, coriander powder, turmeric powder and salt and cook for a few minutes.
1 cup coconut milk	
½ cup oil	Add the fish and tamarind pulp and cook for a few more minutes before adding the coconut milk.
4 green chillies	
2 large onions	Gently stir, add pepper powder and fenugreek powder and remove from fire.
2 tomatoes	
extract of 1 lime-sized tamarind	
juice of 1 lime	
a few curry leaves	*Serve hot with steamed rice.*
salt to taste	

CHETTINAD FISH FRY

Pioneers in trade and finance and experts in the art of using spices, the Chettiars have mastered non-vegetarian curries. The Chettinad fish fry is no exception and Mom used a simple but potent masala to fry the fish a perfect golden brown.

PREP TIME: 15 MIN. | MARINATION TIME: 30 MIN. | COOKING TIME: 20 MIN. | SERVES: 4–6

500 gm fish (seer or pomfret)
½ tsp turmeric powder
1 tsp chilli powder
1 egg white
juice of 1 lime or tamarind extract
3 cups oil
salt to taste

Masala to be Ground
8 dried red chillies
1 tsp cumin seeds
1 tsp fennel seeds
2 tsp coriander seeds
1 tbsp fenugreek seeds
1 tbsp poppy seeds
1 tbsp peppercorns
1-inch piece ginger mashed
1 pod garlic
9–10 curry leaves

Wash and pat the fish dry and slice it (if using pomfrets then don't slice them).
Roast the ingredients for the masala and grind them into a fine paste. Add turmeric, chilli powder, salt, lime juice or tamarind extract and a little oil.
Apply this masala on the fish slices.
Keep aside for 20–30 minutes in the refrigerator.
Apply the egg white on the marinated fish slices.
Heat the oil in a frying pan, add the fish slices one at a time and fry well till golden brown on both sides.

Serve with steamed rice and sambar.

STEAMED FISH IN BANANA LEAVES

If you're a food buff (and even if you're not) who watches what you eat, give this recipe a shot. Just remember not to go overboard on the steaming or the fish will become dry and harder than it's supposed to be.

PREP TIME: 15 MIN. | COOKING TIME: 20 MIN. | SERVES: 4–6

1 kg pomfret	Wash and clean the fish and slice.
1 pod garlic	Rub the pieces with salt, turmeric and lime juice and set aside.
1-inch ginger piece	Wash and roughly chop the coriander and mint leaves.
1 bunch coriander leaves	Cut the green chillies into big pieces.
1 bunch mint leaves	Chop the ginger and garlic roughly. Grind all these to a fine paste.
1 tsp turmeric powder	Mix a little oil into this paste and apply on both sides of the fish slices.
juice of 1 lime or 2 tbsp vinegar	Wrap each piece individually in a banana leaf.
1 coconut grated	Boil water in an idli pot or steamer and carefully place the wrapped fish and steam for 15 to 20 minutes.
3 onions	
8 green chillies	
oil for rubbing	*Serve hot with rice and rasam.*
a few banana leaves	
salt to taste	

PAMBAN FISH CURRY

The Pamban fish market, in Rameswaram, Mother's ancestral home, was her first stop when she arrived there. This huge coastal market with the freshest catches is a sight to behold and a smell to get used to. Although I would hold my nose as I watched her bargain for the best price of fish, the anticipation of her appetising Pamban fish curry would keep me going.

PREP TIME: 20 MIN. | COOKING TIME: 20 MIN. | SERVES: 6–8

1 kg seer fish
(or Indian butter fish or mackerel)
500 gm sambar (small) onions
2 medium-sized tomatoes
2 tbsp red chilli powder
3 tbsp coriander powder
1 tbsp turmeric powder
1 tbsp cumin seeds
3 tbsp poppy seeds
1 tsp black mustard seeds
1 tsp fenugreek seeds
1 tsp peppercorns
2-inch ginger piece
6–8 peeled garlic cloves
1-inch cinnamon stick
4 cloves
4 green cardamoms
4 or 5 green chillies
1 coconut grated
1 lime-sized tamarind
2–3 tbsp oil
a few curry leaves
salt to taste

Wash the fish and rub the salt, turmeric and lime juice on the whole fish, cut into medium-sized pieces and keep aside.

Roast the cumin seeds, peppercorns, coconut, poppy seeds, ginger, a pod of garlic and whole spices and grind to a paste.

Peel the sambar onions and a garlic pod and grind the tomatoes. You can vary the consistency by adding some water.

Heat the oil, add mustard seeds, fenugreek seeds, onions, whole garlic cloves, slit chillies and curry leaves and sauté well. Then add the coarsely grounded tomatoes, turmeric and ground masala and season with salt.

Add the tamarind pulp extract once the masala and tomato are well cooked.

Add some water and cook on slow flame till the curry is thick.

Add the marinated fish and cook till tender.

Serve with plain rice.

FISH SAMBAL

This great traditional Malay dish is another takeaway from the family cook in Singapore. Easy to prepare, it consists of fried whole fish smothered with sambal sauce. Mom always said that the two things needed for a perfect fish fry were seasoning and piping hot oil.

PREP TIME: 10 MIN. | COOKING TIME: 20 MIN. | SERVES: 6-8

1 kg seer fish (any meaty sea fish or small dried fish)
3 tbsp coriander powder
2–4 tbsp chilli powder
1 tsp turmeric powder
1-inch ginger piece
1 pod garlic
1 bunch lemongrass
1 cup coconut milk
3 onions
4 tomatoes
juice of 1 lime
2 tbsp oil
a few coriander leaves
salt to taste

Wash and clean the fish and cut it into slices.

Mix 1 tbsp coriander powder, chilli powder, turmeric, lime juice and some salt and oil.

Rub this masala on the fish and set aside.

Grind the onions with ginger and garlic together. Grind the tomatoes coarsely, tie the lemongrass well.

Heat the oil and fry the fish until it is golden brown. Remove from the stove and keep aside.

Strain the oil, heat it again and add the onion, ginger–garlic paste and sauté well.

Add the ground tomatoes, chilli and coriander powder, turmeric, salt and lemongrass tied together in a bunch.

Sauté well, add coconut milk and cook for a few minutes.

Add the fried fish slowly one by one and cook on slow fire for 5 minutes. You may remove the lemongrass or leave it in the pan for more flavour.

Serve hot with coconut rice or ghee rice.

TAMARIND FISH CURRY

Rich in vitamin B and calcium and containing powerful antioxidant properties, tamarind is generously used in a host of seafood dishes because of its ability to infuse a fruity yet tangy taste. Fresh tamarind pods are available in late spring and early summer seasons in India. All this talk of tamarind reminds me of a childhood visit to my parents' farm in Madurai. On one of our morning walks, we came across a gathering of local women pounding on tamarind pods with wooden sticks. As we stopped to watch, Mom on noticing our curious expressions explained how this was the traditional way to loosen the tamarind pulp before scooping it out of the pod—a process practised to this day.

PREP TIME: 10 MIN. | COOKING TIME: 25 MIN. | SERVES: 6–8

Ingredients	Method
1 kg fish (Indian salmon or any fatty fish)	Wash and clean the fish, and cut into medium-sized pieces. Rub them with some turmeric powder and lime juice.
½ tsp mustard seeds	Peel the onions and garlic.
½ tsp fenugreek seeds	Slit the green chillies.
½ tsp cumin seeds	Cut the tomatoes into eight pieces.
2 tbsp chilli powder	Heat the oil, add the fenugreek seeds, mustard seeds, cumin seeds and curry leaves, and sauté well.
2 tbsp coriander powder	
½ tsp turmeric powder	Add the onions, slit green chillies and whole garlic, sauté till golden brown.
extract of 1 lime-sized tamarind	
1 grated medium-sized coconut or 3–4 cups coconut milk	Then add the tomatoes, coriander powder, chilli powder, turmeric and salt. Mix and sauté well.
1 pod garlic	Add some water and boil for a few minutes.
juice of 1 lime	Then add the coconut milk and stir well.
3 tomatoes	Add the tamarind pulp into the gravy and boil for 5 minutes. Then add the fish slices.
20 sambar (small) onions	
4–6 green chillies	Cook for 10 to 15 minutes on low flame.
3 tbsp oil	
a few curry leaves	
salt to taste	

Serve with steamed rice.

Note:
Do not stir once the fish is added to the gravy.

STUFFED FISH MASALA

It was love at first bite at a restaurant in Hyderabad and Dad tells us that Mom sweet-talked the chef into divulging his precious recipe.

PREP TIME: 15 MIN. | COOKING TIME: 10 MIN. | SERVES: 6

6 medium pomfrets or mackerel
3 tbsp garlic paste
3–4 tbsp red chilli powder
1 tsp cumin powder
½ tsp turmeric powder
¼ cup vinegar or lemon juice
1 tbsp tamarind pulp
salt to taste
oil

Wash and clean the fish well. Slit it from the side for stuffing.
Rub the fish with salt and lemon juice and keep aside.
Grind all the ingredients with vinegar/lemon juice.
Stuff the fish with the masala and rub some on the outside as well.
Heat oil and fry till golden brown and cooked.

Serve with rice.

FISH CURRY IN COCONUT MILK

This richer, creamier version of Mother's favourite fish curry is a classic. The coconut milk adds a slightly sweet taste to this otherwise spicy curry. Mom preferred using seer fish because the texture is just perfect for this curry. But you could use any other meaty fish.

PREP TIME: 20 MIN. | COOKING TIME: 30 MIN. | SERVES: 6–8

1 kg seer fish	Wash, clean and cut the fish, rub lemon juice and salt, keep aside.
4 tbsp ginger–garlic paste	Cut the onions and tomatoes, slit the green chillies and break dry red chillies into medium-sized pieces. Chop the ginger finely. Grind the cashew nuts into a fine paste.
1-inch ginger piece	
2 tbsp red chilli powder	
1 tsp pepper powder	Extract 2 cups of thick and 2 cups of thin milk from the grated coconut. Heat the oil, fry the onions, ginger–garlic paste, green chillies and dry red chillies, reduce the heat and add the pepper powder, turmeric and chopped tomatoes.
1 tsp turmeric powder	
2 onions	
3–4 green chillies	
3–4 red chillies	Sauté well. Add the chilli powder and salt.
1 coconut	Add the thin coconut milk and bring it to a boil. Cook on low heat till the curry is half thick then add the fish.
4 tomatoes	
10 cashew nuts	Cook for 5 minutes on slow fire.
juice of 1 whole lime	Add the thick coconut milk, cashew nut and curry leaves. Cook on low flame for 10 minutes till tender.
2 tbsp oil	
a few curry leaves	
salt to taste	*Serve with string hoppers or appams.*

DRIED FISH PORIYAL

This typically South Indian coastal dish works for those who have an adventurous culinary side or love dried fish.

PREP TIME: 40 MIN. | COOKING TIME: 10 MIN. | SERVES: 6–8

500 gm dried fish
500 gm small onions
2 tbsp oil
3 pods garlic
6 green chillies
1 tsp turmeric powder
1 tsp chilli powder
a few coriander leaves
a few curry leaves
salt to taste

Soak the dried fish in water for about 30 minutes, then rinse and wash well.

Make sure that all the sand and excess salt is removed. Add turmeric and chilli powder and set the fish aside for at least 10 minutes, the longer the better.

Chop the onions and green chillies finely and slice the garlic.

Heat the oil and fry with the curry leaves and very little salt.

Add the washed dried fish to the fried onions, mix well and cook till soft.

Garnish with coriander leaves.

Note:
You can also use 15 full cloves of garlic and 2 big onions instead of small onions.

FISH PUTTU WITH MORINGA LEAVES

For this Chettinad puttu recipe, Mom used shark fish but you could use any white meaty fish like Indian salmon. It is fluffy and soft and accompanied by moringa leaves makes a wonderful meal for both children and older people and its nutritious value makes it a superfood for nursing mothers.

PREP TIME: 30 MIN. | COOKING TIME: 20 MIN. | SERVES: 6–8

1 kg shark fish	Completely remove the head, tail and skin of the fish and cut it into slices.
4 big onions	
10 green chillies	Wash well and boil the fish in a little water with turmeric and salt.
1 tbsp ginger–garlic paste	Remove it from the water and let it cool.
1 tbsp red chilli powder	Break the meat into tiny pieces making sure the bones are removed.
1 tbsp turmeric powder	Mince the onions and green chillies finely.
3 tbsp coriander powder	Take a pan and fry the onions and green chillies well and add the fish.
1 cup scraped coconut	Mix in ginger–garlic paste, chilli, coriander and turmeric powder and salt to taste.
1 cup chopped moringa leaves	
2 sprigs curry leaves	Keep stirring on low flame for 10 minutes.
½ bunch chopped coriander leaves	Finally add the coconut flakes, moringa leaves and coriander leaves and stir fry for 10 minutes.
2 tbsp oil	
salt to taste	

Serve with rice.

PRAWNS AND GREEN PEAS MASALA

Perhaps it's the complexity of flavours of peas and prawns, but this not-so-common combination of never failed to lift my spirits.

PREP TIME: 15 MIN. | COOKING TIME: 20 MIN. | SERVES: 4–6

1 kg medium-sized prawns
500 gm green peas
1 tbsp coriander powder
2 tbsp chilli powder
1 tsp garam masala powder
½ tsp turmeric powder
2 tsp cumin powder
3 tbsp oil
2 tsp ginger–garlic paste
3 onions
3 tomatoes
2–4 green chillies
4 cloves
4 green cardamoms
1-inch 4 cinnamon sticks
a few curry leaves
a few coriander leaves
a few mint leaves
salt to taste

Wash, devein and drain the prawns well.
Heat the oil and fry the finely chopped onions and the whole spices for a few minutes, add the ginger–garlic paste.
Sauté well then add the finely chopped green chillies and finely chopped tomatoes. Sauté.
Add all the masalas and cook till the oil separates.
Then add the prawns and green peas. Add 1 cup water and salt, cover and cook on slow fire till dry.
Garnish with curry leaves, coriander leaves and mint leaves.

Serve the dish with idiyappam, rice or chapattis.

Note:
Lima beans or snow peas and potatoes can also be added.
You could also substitute prawns for minced mutton or chicken.

PRAWN CURRY

You know a good dish when the kids plead for more and this prawn curry fits that bill perfectly. Our brother's friends would call to ask 'Aunty', our mom, to make that 'mind-blowing' prawn curry.

PREP TIME: 10 MIN. | COOKING TIME: 15 MIN. | SERVES: 6–8

1 kg medium/large prawns
2 tbsp chilli powder
2 tsp cumin powder
1 tsp turmeric powder
3 tbsp ginger–garlic paste
1 tbsp lemon juice
1 cup coconut milk
2 onions
4 tomatoes
2 tbsp oil
a few curry leaves
a few coriander leaves
salt to taste

Wash and devein the prawns. Then rub them with salt and lemon juice to take the smell out and keep them aside.

Chop the onions and tomatoes.

Heat the oil, fry the onions and the ginger–garlic paste.

Sauté well, then add the tomatoes, turmeric, chilli powder, cumin powder and salt and sauté for 5 minutes.

Add the coconut milk and prawns, and then add the curry leaves and cook on low flame till thick.

Garnish with coriander leaves.

Serve with steamed rice or bread.

SPICY PRAWN MASALA

Saturday afternoons and debates on politics and family issues all required the regular intervention of the spicy prawn masala. Conversations would cease until every single prawn was devoured, and more were welcome.

PREP TIME: 10 MIN. | COOKING TIME: 15 MIN. | SERVES: 6–8

1 kg medium or large prawns
3–4 tbsp chilli powder
1 tsp turmeric powder
3 tbsp ginger–garlic paste
2 tsp lemon juice
1 cup coconut milk
4 large onions
5 tomatoes
2 tbsp oil
a few coriander leaves
a few curry leaves
salt to taste

Wash and devein the prawns, rub them with lemon juice and salt and keep aside.

Grind the onions, tomatoes and coriander leaves separately.

Heat the oil, add the onion paste and ginger–garlic paste and sauté till golden brown.

Add the tomato paste, turmeric, chilli powder and salt and sauté well for 10 minutes.

Add the prawns and coconut milk and cook on medium flame till semi-dry.

Add the curry leaves and coriander leaves.

Note:
You can add green peas.

PRAWN KURMA

A sensory delight, these exotic prawns are simmered in spices and coconut milk. Make the masala separately, add the coconut milk and then add the prawns once the masala is ready. Always let the prawns cook on low flame so that they remain tender.

PREP TIME: 10 MIN. | COOKING TIME: 20 MIN. | SERVES: 6–8

1 kg medium-sized prawns
1 tsp ginger paste
2 tbsp white vinegar or tamarind extract
2 tbsp coriander powder
2 tsp chilli powder
1 tsp turmeric powder
2 tsp lemon juice
1 cup coconut milk
1 large onion
7 garlic cloves
2 tomatoes
1 tsp peppercorns
2 tbsp oil
a few curry leaves
a few coriander leaves
salt to taste

Clean, devein and wash prawns.
Rub with salt and lemon juice and keep aside.
Cut the onion and slice the garlic cloves.
Mix all the spices in a bowl with vinegar or tamarind extract.
Heat the oil and add the onion, curry leaves and garlic. Fry till golden brown then add the mixed spices and sauté for 5 minutes.
Add the tomatoes, salt and peppercorns and simmer for 5 minutes.
Add the coconut milk; when it boils add the prawns and cook till the is coated thick and curry.
Garnish with coriander.

Serve with rice.

GOONG PAD (fried prawns)

The Strait of Malacca, a trade centre since long, had a huge mix of nationalities and therefore a variety of cuisines to discover. Mom would often visit her father who owned mines in Ipoh, and her nanny who was from Ipoh would often join them. It was she who taught Mom how to make these spectacular fried prawns in true Malay style.

PREP TIME: 15 MIN. | MARINATION TIME: 30 MIN. | COOKING TIME: 10 MIN. | SERVES: 4

500 gm medium/large-sized prawns
2 tbsp lemongrass
2 tbsp oil
2 tsp coriander roots
2 tsp pepper
2 tsp lemon juice
½ tsp shrimp paste (optional)
¼ tsp nutmeg powder
¼ cup coconut milk
¾ cup rice flour
1-inch ginger piece
6 garlic cloves
2 onions
6 fresh red chillies
a few spring onions
salt to taste

Wash and remove the shells leaving the tails and devein the prawns. Drain well.

Cut the onions, red chillies, ginger, garlic, lemongrass, coriander roots finely. Sauté these and leave aside to cool, and then grind them to a smooth paste, adding the coconut milk.

Mix well with the shrimp paste, nutmeg powder and lemon juice.

Add this paste to the prawns and keep them aside for 30 minutes.

Mix flour, pepper and salt.

Coat the prawns with the flour.

Heat oil in a wok and add the prawns.

Cook till it curls.

Place them on paper.

Serve hot.

PRAWNS IN THEEYAL MASALA

From the 'land of spices' to Mom's kitchen, this recipe includes a special masala called theeyal, which is the key ingredient used in Kerala cuisine. Mom would stand patiently over the stove, humming away whilst the ingredients slow roasted in the pan. It was more love than the effort that made the theeyal masala turn out just perfect.

PREP TIME: 20 MIN. | COOKING TIME: 20 MIN. | SERVES: 4–6

500 gm medium-sized prawns
250 gm shallots
5 tsp theeyal masala (recipe given below)
½ tsp black mustard seeds
½ coconut grated
5 dried red chillies
pulp of a lime-sized tamarind
2 tbsp oil
a few curry leaves
salt to taste

Theeyal Masala
(roasted coconut with spices)
1 tbsp coriander seeds
1 tbsp cumin seeds
1 tsp fenugreek seeds
½ tsp turmeric powder
½ grated coconut
20 peppercorns
5 dried red chillies
10 sambar onions

Wash, devein and clean the prawns and set them aside.
Cut the onions into halves.
Heat the oil, add mustard seeds and dried red chillies and sauté for a few minutes; add the onions and sauté till golden brown. Then add the curry leaves.
Add turmeric, salt, tamarind and the theeyal masala to the masala.
Add the pulp to the pan and bring it to a boil.
Add the prawns and cook for a few minutes.
Cook on low flame for about 10 minutes till the gravy is medium thick.

Serve with steamed rice.

Theeyal Masala
Roast the theeyal masala ingredients and grind them to a paste. If prepared without the coconut and sambar onions it can be stored in an airtight bottle for a year.

SPICY CHILLI CRAB

When Dad was posted in Odisha for a few years, he would come home bearing live crabs as gifts. To little girls, live crabs are not cuddly toys and so you would find me scrambling up the sofa and shrieking at the sight of them but only until they were covered in beautiful spices and cooked to perfection by Mom.

PREP TIME: 20 MIN. | COOKING TIME: 50 MIN. | SERVES: 6–8

1 kg crabs	Soak the dried red chillies for 10 minutes. Grind them into a paste.
250 gm dried prawns	Wash, clean and cut the crabs.
2 spring onions (green ends only)	Grind 5 onions, ginger and garlic into a paste.
2-inch ginger piece	Grind the tomatoes.
6 cloves garlic	Finely cut 1 onion.
juice of 2 limes	Heat oil in a deep pan, fry the finely cut onion, add the onion and ginger–garlic paste, sauté well.
100 gm dried red chillies	
1 egg	Add the tomato paste, salt and sugar, sauté and then add the chilli paste. Cook on low flame.
6 onions	
5 tomatoes	Add the lime juice and cook till the oil separates.
1 tsp sugar	Add the crab pieces and dark soy sauce, cook till done.
1 tsp dark soy sauce	Soak the dried prawns in water for 2–3 minutes, wash well and then squeeze out the water.
Chinese parsley	
1 cup fish/chicken stock	In a pan, fry the dried prawns crispy.
2 tbsp oil	Add the fried prawns to the crab gravy.
salt to taste	Beat the egg and scramble it. Add it to the crab dish and mix well; stir in chopped spring onions. Garnish with chopped Chinese parsley.

Serve hot with steamed rice.

SINGAPORE-STYLE SPICY CRAB CURRY

From her Singapore days of learning from the local cook, this authentic crab curry showed Mom's talent for picking up the local flavours and styles of cooking.

PREP TIME: 20 MIN. | COOKING TIME: 20 MIN. | SERVES: 6–8

1 kg crabs
4 garlic pods
1 small ginger piece
2 tbsp oil
1 tsp dark soy sauce
1 tbsp sugar
½ cup water
1 cup coconut milk
6 red chillies
6 green chillies
1 green capsicum
9 spring onions
small bunch of lemongrass
salt to taste

Wash and clean the crabs, cut into a few pieces, crack the claws.
Chop the garlic and ginger, slit the chillies lengthwise. Soak the red chillies for 5 minutes and grind them to a paste.
Heat 1 tbsp oil in a wok to smoking point, add the crabs and stir well till the shells turn red and the meat is white.
Remove from the fire and keep aside. Discard the oil.
Heat oil in another pan, add the chopped ginger and garlic and red chilli paste, sauté for a few minutes and add the slit green chillies.
Add crabs, soy sauce, coconut milk, lemongrass, chopped green capsicum, salt and water, simmer till the crab is done.
Add the spring onions and mix well.

Serve with plain rice.

CRAB MEAT PUTTU

Crab puttu is a delicacy that seafood enthusiasts would love to try for a change from the usual curries. I love this dish for its ease of preparing and its light but fantastic flavour.

PREP TIME: 30 MIN. | COOKING TIME: 20 MIN. | SERVES: 6

1 kg crabs
4 big onions
10–15 green chillies
1 tbsp ginger–garlic paste
1 tbsp chilli powder
1 tbsp coriander powder
1 tbsp turmeric powder
½ cup coriander leaves
1 tbsp oil
salt to taste

Clean the crabs. Plunge the crab head first into boiling water; if you have too much water, ladle out excess and discard. Cover the pan and start timing. When the water resumes boiling, reduce the heat to a simmer. Cook the crabs for 15 minutes.

Remove the meat and shred it.

Cut the onions and the green chillies finely.

Fry the onions till brown, add green chillies and fry.

Add crab meat, all the masalas and mix well.

Keep on low flame, add coriander leaves and stir fry for 10 minutes.

Serve with rice.

STUFFED CRAB SHELLS

Sibling rivalry over stuffed crab shells shows just how much this dish is worth. Ravenous after a long day at school, I headed straight to the kitchen to find out what that divine smell was. Voila! Two gorgeously baked stuffed crab shells lay await in the oven. Unable to resist, I devoured them both and ran off to play, returning only to find my older sister Anita ready to throw the biggest fit ever. When it dawned on me that I had eaten her portion of the baked crab without realizing it, I sheepishly and fearfully, admitted my mistake and apologized. A really miffed Anita took a while to get over it and a few months at least to forgive me. But my very amused father to this day never fails to laugh and joke about this incident when we eat Mom's baked crab together.

PREP TIME: 60 MIN. | COOKING TIME: 30 MIN. | SERVES: 4

4 medium-sized crabs
2 onions
1 beaten egg
6 garlic flakes
½ cup grated cheese
½ cup coconut milk
½ cup breadcrumbs
2 tbsp cornflour (or multi-purpose flour)
2 tsp pepper powder
5 tsp coriander/mint leaves
125 gm bacon/lean pork
1-inch ginger piece
2 tbsp oil
salt to taste

Cut the onions, ginger and garlic, mince the bacon/lean pork, chop the coriander and mint leaves finely.

Cook the crabs in boiling water and carefully remove the top shells and set aside.

Extract all the meat from the body and claws and shred finely.

Fry the chopped onions, garlic and ginger.

Remove the fried onions and garlic–ginger masala and mix this with the minced bacon, egg, cornflour, coconut milk, pepper and coriander/mint leaves.

Butter the crab shells and transfer the mixture into the empty crab shells.

Sprinkle some cheese and breadcrumbs on the mixture. Place in a steamer for 30 minutes. Remove and set aside.

Before serving, heat the oil until it smokes, deep fry or bake the stuffed shells till golden brown.

Note:
If baking, do so at 160 °C or 230 °F for 30 minutes.

CRAB MASALA

Hand-picked crabs, fresh from the trawlers, cooked to perfection, with a coating of my mother's heavenly masala. I could never have enough of this delectable dish.

PREP TIME: 15 MIN. | COOKING TIME: 25 MIN. | SERVES: 6

6 crabs	Wash and clean the crabs.
paste of 3 onions	Heat the oil and fry the onion paste and ginger–garlic paste. Sauté till golden brown, then add the chopped tomatoes.
4 tomatoes	
2 tsp ginger paste	Sauté and then add the chilli powder, cumin powder, coriander powder, turmeric and salt.
2 tsp garlic paste	
1 tbsp turmeric powder	Add the coconut milk and the curry leaves. Cover and cook for 10 minutes.
2 tsp chilli powder	
2 tbsp cumin powder	Add the crabs. Mix and cook on low flame till the masala becomes semi-dry.
2 tbsp coriander powder	
2 tbsp oil	Garnish with chopped coriander leaves.
½ cup coconut milk	
a few curry leaves	*Serve with steamed rice or bread.*
a few coriander leaves	
salt to taste	

SQUID MASALA

For those who like eating squid, this is a delightful preparation where the combination of tamarind, chilli paste and sugar renders a flavourful complexity to it.

PREP TIME: 10 MIN. | COOKING TIME: 30 MIN. | SERVES: 4–6

500 gm squids	Wash and clean the squids. Cut them into rings; keep aside.
4 tbsp tamarind pulp	Slice the onions finely.
3 tsp red chilli paste	Heat the oil and add the sliced onions and chopped garlic. Fry till golden brown.
2–3 lemongrass	
6 lime leaves	Add the green and red chillies and the red chilli paste and sauté for a few minutes.
½ cup grated coconut for extracting coconut milk	
2 tbsp grated coconut for roasting	Grind the garlic cloves, onions, turmeric powder, dried chillies, coriander powder and cumin powder.
½ tsp turmeric powder	Heat the oil in a wok and fry the ground ingredients till fragrant.
1½ tsp cumin powder	Add 2 tbsp of grated coconut to the roast.
½ tsp sugar	Add 2 cups of warm water to the grated coconut and extract 3 cups of coconut milk. Add this extract to the roasted ingredients. Add lemongrass and lime leaves. Cook till the curry is of thick consistency.
2 onions	
3 green chillies	
3 dried red chillies	Add the squid, water, salt and sugar, stir well and then add the tamarind pulp. Cook till semi-dry.
10 chopped garlic cloves	
2 tbsp oil	
salt to taste	

Serve with rice.

Note:
Do not overcook the squids or they will become rubbery.

BAKES, ROASTS & GRILLS

We knew a treat was in the oven when we saw Mom pouring over 'The Big Blue Book' where all her recipes and notes from her time at Le Cordon Bleu were stored. Dad's favourite was the glazed roast chicken, my sister and I voted for the mac and cheese, and my brother picked the perfectly baked cauliflower. Arguments over our favourite picks only fuelled her enthusiasm and we ended up with a table runner lined with bakes and sauces that looked like they were waiting for a French chef's nod—our delighted exclamations served just as well!

The recipes in this chapter are a medley of baked delights that serve as homely, one-pot comfort food.

GRILLED ORANGE CHICKEN

Light on the belly and bursting with flavours, this grilled orange chicken is so easy to make. The trick lies in getting the marinade just right. Serve it with creamy mashed potatoes and a few sautéed veggies like broccoli, baby corn and bell pepper and you're good to go.

PREP TIME: 15 MIN. | MARINATION TIME: 4–5 HRS. or OVERNIGHT | COOKING TIME: 60 MIN. | SERVES: 2

2 chicken breasts (skinless)
3 tsp garlic paste
1 tbsp mixed herbs
2 tbsp honey
¼ tsp salt
1 tbsp chilli powder
1 cup orange juice (freshly squeezed)

Rinse the chicken breasts and pat them dry with a paper towel.
Place them in a 9 x 13-inch baking dish.
Pour the orange juice over the chicken breasts.
In a small bowl, combine garlic, herbs, honey, salt and chilli powder and rub the mixture onto the chicken.
Marinate the chicken in the refrigerator for 3–5 hours or time permitting.
Place the breasts on a plate and set the marinade aside.
Grill each side of chicken on a barbecue until the chicken is cooked.
Cook the extra marinade gravy on a low flame for 10–15 minutes.
Pour it on the grilled chicken and serve.

ROAST CHICKEN

Sunday brunches often began with the delicate but sweet and spicy aroma of a herbed and well-roasted golden brown chicken, crispy on the outside and tender and juicy on the inside. Mom's portions were large and Monday lunches were a treat with roast chicken sandwiches in our lunch boxes. This no-fuss recipe is sure to find a favourite spot on your weekly menu.

PREP TIME: 10 MIN. | MARINATION TIME: OVERNIGHT | COOKING TIME: 105 MIN. | SERVES: 4–6

1 whole chicken with skin 1 pod crushed garlic 3 tbsp sambar masala 1 tbsp crushed pepper 1 tsp red chilli flakes 1 tbsp thyme 1 tbsp fresh rosemary juice of 1 lime 2 tbsp honey 1 tbsp apple cider vinegar 1 tbsp oil or butter 2 sprigs fresh rosemary salt to taste	Mix all the ingredients together and rub on the outside and inside of the chicken. Marinate for 2–3 hours. Preheat the oven to 350 °F or 175 °C. Add the fresh rosemary and bake the chicken uncovered for 1 hour 10 minutes. Cover with foil and allow to cool down before serving.

BELL PEPPERS STUFFED WITH MINCE

Summer holidays in Bangalore would have the grandchildren curiously hovering around Mom in the kitchen cooking up stories, menus and food. It was one of the tête-à-têtes in the kitchen with her granddaughter that led to this combination of green pepper and mince—now a favourite with all of us. It all comes together quite nicely with cheese being a binder. The lemon rind, however, is the ingredient that elevates the unique flavour of this dish.

COOKING TIME: 45 MIN. | SERVES: 4

4 bell peppers 3 cloves garlic 250 gm mince (beef, mutton, lamb or chicken) 1-inch ginger piece 1 tbsp oil 2 spring onions 1 cup cheese (mozzarella or cheddar) 1 celery stick 1 lemon 1 onion 3 green chillies salt to taste 1 tsp butter	Wash the meat and drain. Chop the onion, garlic, ginger, spring onions, green chillies and celery stick finely. Grate the lemon rind. Cut the bell peppers into half and scoop out the seeds. Rub the butter inside and outside. Heat oil, add the onions, ginger–garlic paste and salt, sauté and add the green chillies along with the mince. Cook till the mince is cooked, add the spring onions and celery stick and the lemon rind. Cook till dry. Spoon this mixture into the bell pepper halves.

STUFFED BAKED TOMATOES

On a rainy day in Bangalore the weather turns super cool and perfect for these piping hot flavourful tomatoes. My mother hand-picked perfect large tomatoes for this recipe and this was a sure winner for my sisters.

COOKING TIME: 45 MIN. | SERVES: 8

8 large tomatoes
500 gm minced meat (chicken or beef or lamb) or 1 cup cottage cheese (vegetarian option)
8 mushrooms
1 tbsp oil
2 large onions
2 tbsp dry wine/sherry
1 bunch coriander leaves
2 tbsp soy sauce
5 water chestnuts (optional)
1 tbsp all-purpose flour
1 cup grated cheese (parmesan or cheddar)
50 gm pine nuts
salt and pepper to taste

Wash the mushrooms, pat them dry and cut finely.
Chop the tomatoes and onions. Wash the mince and drain. Chop the water chestnuts and nuts.
Blend the flour with 3 tbsp water, making sure there are no lumps.
Cut the tomatoes in halves and scoop out the flesh. Put the pulp aside.
Heat the oil, add the onions and meat, fry till brown and the meat is cooked.
Stir in the mushrooms, nuts, soy sauce and dry wine/sherry, and cook for 5 minutes. Remove from fire and set aside.
In the pan, add the tomato pulp and flour paste and cook for 2 minutes. Add the cooked meat and stir well.
Spoon the mixture into the tomato halves and garnish with grated cheese and coriander leaves.

Note:
For the vegetarians, add the cottage cheese last after removing from flame.
Bake in a preheated oven for 20 to 25 minutes at 180 °C / 350 °F/ gas mark 4.

BAKED CAULIFLOWER IN WHITE SAUCE

It was on a lunch date with Mom at Bangalore's Woody's that our brother discovered his all-time favourite dish–the cheesy baked cauliflower. Mom noticed the way his face lit up with excitement when the cauliflower bake was brought to the table and she made her own version.

COOKING TIME: 45 MIN. | SERVES: 8

1 kg cauliflower
1 beaten egg
1 tsp pepper powder
½ tsp chilli powder
2 tbsp all-purpose flour
6 tbsp milk
100 gm cheese grated (parmesan or cheddar)
salt to taste

For White Sauce
(for the detailed recipe, refer to the Spices, Stocks & Masalas section)
1½ tbsp all-purpose flour
2 cups milk
1 tsp pepper
salt to taste
1 tbsp butter
4 tbsp grated cheese (parmesan or cheddar)

Cut the cauliflower into small pieces.
Boil the cauliflower with a little salt or vinegar in 1 cup of water.
Remove and drain the water, then add ½ tsp of pepper, salt and cheese.
To make the white sauce mix all the ingredients and cook on low flame, keep stirring all the time.
Then mix the white sauce with the cauliflower.
Grease a baking dish and pour the mixture into the dish.
Mix the flour, beaten egg, milk, chilli powder and salt and pour this mix over the cauliflower.
Bake in a moderately hot oven (140 °C or 284 °F) for approximately 20 minutes till the crust turns an even golden brown.

Serve with garlic bread.

MOM's SHEPHERD's PIE

Mom's Shepherd's Pie conjures up memories of rainy nights, tons of chit-chat and quirky board games. Ever so often, my brother or my dad would playfully try to distract Mom with something or the other so they could win, without ever managing to succeed. Peals of laughter and a steaming Shepherd's Pie in the backdrop are memories of the good times.

COOKING TIME: 60 MIN. | SERVES: 4

1½ cups penne or conchiglie (shell) pasta
1½ cups mince (chicken or mutton)
4 tomatoes
3 onions
½-inch cinnamon stick
6 green chillies
½ cup cheddar cheese
2 cloves
3 tbsp chopped garlic
1 bay leaf
3 tbsp butter
a few parsley leaves
1 tsp red chilli powder
2 tbsp coriander powder
a few coriander leaves
salt to taste

Wash and drain the mince. Cook the pasta, drain and set aside.

Finely chop the onions, tomatoes, green chillies and coriander leaves and powder.

Grate the cheese. Break the bay leaf.

Heat the butter, add the cinnamon and cloves, bay leaf, green chillies and sauté well.

Add the onions. Fry well and add the tomatoes, sauté for a few minutes. Add salt to taste.

Add the red chilli powder and coriander powder, sauté for 10 minutes.

Add the mince mix, fry well and cook for 20 minutes with a little water till dry.

Remove and set aside.

Add the cooked pasta, mix well.

Butter a baking dish, put the mince in it, and garnish it with chopped parsley leaves.

Then layer the pasta, spread some butter, sprinkle shredded cheddar cheese and bake at 175 °C or 350 °F until the cheese is golden brown.

Serve hot.

Note:
You can add the mashed potatoes as a final layer, spread some butter, then sprinkle grated cheese and bake.

CHEESE STUFFED BELL PEPPERS

This tangy, delectable stuffed capsicum from Mom's repertoire is for all the vegetarians out there. Mustard oil (optional if you're not used to its strong flavour) and raw mango powder give this dish that extra kick.

COOKING TIME: 40 MIN. | SERVES: 4–6

3 big red, green and yellow bell peppers	Boil and mash the potatoes in a separate bowl.
3 green chillies	Heat a pan with a little ghee or oil.
1 tbsp mustard oil (optional)	Add the cumin powder and turmeric powder.
4 large potatoes	Sauté for 1 minute and add the green chillies.
½ tsp cumin powder	Add the mashed potatoes and spices. Mix well and cook for 2 minutes on low flame.
½ tsp red chilli powder	Mix the chopped coriander and set aside to cool at room temperature.
2 tsp coriander powder	Cut the top part of the bell peppers very carefully and remove the seeds.
½ tsp raw mango powder	Stuff the bell pepper with the potato mixture and the feta and grated cheese, together alternating the layers. Finish with a layer of feta and grated cheese on top.
½ tsp turmeric powder	
1 tsp dried oregano	
1 cup grated parmesan cheese	
1 cup crumbled feta cheese	Add oil in a wok and heat to smoking point.
a few coriander leaves	Place the bell peppers in the wok and cover and cook for 10–15 minutes until they are soft and tender.
salt to taste	

Note:
Preheat the oven to 350 °F or 175 °C. Use an ovenproof pot with a tight-fitting lid; add 1 cup water. Cover, bake for approximately 45 minutes until the peppers are tender. You can also add cooked minced chicken or turkey.

OLD ENGLISH CASSEROLE

Whenever Mom got nostalgic about her days in England, we got to wolf down this perfect winter dish. Cold nights were not wasted in any way.

COOKING TIME: 60 MIN. | SERVES: 4

2 kg chicken breasts	Wash and cut the chicken, rub salt and pepper powder well.
5 strips bacon fat	Cut the onions and bacon fat or strips.
1 tbsp all-purpose flour	Mix the flour with water.
1 cup sliced carrot	Heat the bacon fat or strips. In a heavy pan, add the onions and sauté well.
1 tsp pepper powder	
1 cup boiled peas	Add the chicken breasts and brown on both sides, till they are brown.
1 tsp Worcester sauce	Add the carrot and green peas.
2 onions	Add the flour and mix well.
2 cups chicken stock	Add the Worcester sauce and enough chicken stock to moisten the gravy so that the pan is not dry.
1 tsp salt	

Cover and reduce the heat.

Cook for 30 minutes or until the chicken is tender.

Shake the pan occasionally so that the pan is not dry and add more chicken stock if necessary.

STUFFED ROAST CHICKEN

This caramelised and glazed roast chicken is the perfect centrepiece to dress up your dining table during Christmas or Easter.

PREP TIME: 15 MIN. | COOKING TIME: 2 HRS. | SERVES: 4–6

1 kg chicken
1 tbsp ginger–garlic paste
1 tbsp dark soy sauce

For Stuffing
½ cup water chestnuts cubed
¾ cup shelled green peas
3 chopped tomatoes
¼ cup groundnuts soaked for 2 hrs
4 bread slices cut into cubes
½ tsp powdered peppercorns
3-cm cinnamon stick powdered
a pinch of nutmeg powder
2–3 tbsp ghee
salt to taste

Slit the chicken in the centre.
Clean and remove all the spare parts (only keep the heart and liver for stuffing).
Wash well and pat it dry. Apply the ginger–garlic paste and soy sauce on to the chicken.
Keep it aside and marinate for 2 hours.

For Stuffing
Wash the water chestnuts and chop them.
Heat oil in a deep pan and fry the bread cubes till golden brown.
Remove the bread cubes and add the water chestnuts, green peas and soaked groundnuts (drain water). Keep stirring. Add water if required.
If you're using the liver and heart then add them with the chestnuts.
Add the nutmeg powder, pepper and cinnamon powder. Cover and cook till done.
Add the tomatoes. After all are well fried, keep the pan aside and let it cool.
Add the bread croutons and mix well.

Method for Baking
Put the stuffing into the chicken and stitch it.
Heat a heavy pan and add 2 tbsp sugar, caramelise it and let it cool.
Put 2 tbsp ghee in a baking dish and mace the chicken.
Bake it for half an hour at 180 °C or 260 °F.
Turn the chicken now and then brush it with a prepared caramelised sugar syrup.
The chicken should look golden brown. If needed use ghee during baking.

RICE & NOODLES

One bowl of rice sits unassumingly at every Indian family dining table ready to accompany whichever dish makes it to the table for the meal. And so it sat at ours too, only Mother always had a plethora of interesting recipes that spruced up the rice to be more than just an accompaniment; even a meal by itself. Between lemon rice, tamarind rice and all the various biryanis, meals in Indian households and ours too never reached a stalemate.

Mom loved making and eating noodles too, and she could stir up some pretty scrumptious ones. I thought bringing these to your table would bring variety and cheer, especially to the kids who almost always find noodles an exciting fare.

Food, in the end, in our own tradition
is something holy
  It's not about nutrients and calories
    It's about sharing
      It's about honesty
        It's about identity

—Louise Fresco

LAYERED MUTTON DUM BIRYANI

This elaborate and classic dum biryani was a special treat at home with the fragrance of masalas and caramelised onions wafting through the house and the happy memories coming to my mind as I write down this recipe.

COOKING TIME: 2 HRS. | SERVES: 6

1 kg mutton cut into big pieces
4 cups basmati rice
1 cup cooking oil
1 cup ghee
3 big onions
4 medium-sized tomatoes
3 green chillies
1 cup coriander leaves
½ cup mint leaves
juice of 1 large lime
10 cardamoms, cloves and cinnamon sticks
a pinch of saffron
1 tsp red chilli powder
¼ tsp turmeric powder
500 gm sour curd
1 tbsp ginger–garlic paste
½ cup milk
salt to taste

PART I

Clean and wash the rice and keep aside.

Wash the mutton and keep aside.

Slice the onions long and thin.

Heat the oil and ghee together, add the onions and fry till golden brown.

Add the cloves, cardamoms, cinnamon sticks and fry for 2 minutes.

Add the ginger–garlic paste, whole green chillies and fry for 2 minutes.

Add the mutton pieces and stir till the meat turns whitish.

Add the chopped tomatoes, mint leaves, coriander leaves, red chilli powder and turmeric and sauté for 10 minutes. Add salt, lime juice and beaten curd.

Cover, lower the heat and let it simmer. Keep stirring often to ensure the meat doesn't stick to the bottom of the pan.

The broth is ready when the oil floats on top, it will take 45 minutes to 1 hour.

Drain the oil from the broth and keep aside.

In a large deep vessel, heat 12 cups of water with 2 tsp salt.

When the water begins to boil add the rice, cook till three-fourths done, drain the rice and cool.

Divide the rice into 2 parts and the mutton into 3 parts. Put a layer of mutton, then a layer of rice, repeat the process and end with a layer of mutton.

Pour all the drained oil over the biryani preparation and on the sides too.

Soak saffron in milk and pour over the biryani.

PART II

Cover the vessel with a wet cloth. Put a tight-fitting lid on top.

Place a griddle over low flame and place the vessel over it.

After 10 minutes, open the lid and check if the biryani is full of steam. Switch off and cover the biryani with a lid.

SOFIYANI CHICKEN BIRYANI

This lesser-known, lightly spiced and lower in calories than the usual biryanis supposedly from the Nizam's kitchen is a hidden gem as biryani lovers will discover.

COOKING TIME: 90 MIN. | SERVES: 4

500 gm chicken
500 gm basmati rice
100 gm dry figs
1 cup ghee
3 large tomatoes
1 small lime
1 cup milk
salt to taste

Mix for the Marinade:
500 ml (2 ½ cups) curd
2 tbsp ginger–garlic paste
1 tbsp chilli powder
1 tbsp garam masala powder
1 tbsp almond powder
3 potatoes cubed and fried
a few strands of saffron
¼ tsp turmeric powder
50 gm coriander leaves chopped
6 green chillies slit lengthwise
salt to taste
Marinate the chicken with the above ingredients for 1 hour

Marinate the chicken for 1 hour.

Heat the ghee, add the tempering and fry for 1 minute. Add raw, washed basmati rice and salt and cook lightly. Keep aside.

Slice the 3 tomatoes thickly and slit the 6 green chillies lengthwise. Keep 100 gm dry figs, 2 onions fried crisp and powdered.

½ cup coriander leaves chopped and juice of 1 small lime and 1 cup milk.

Line a heavy-bottomed pan with double foil. Arrange the thickly sliced tomatoes to cover the base. Place the marinated chicken over it. Arrange the green chillies, dried figs and two-thirds of the white rice over it. Colour the remaining rice yellow with saffron in milk and spread over it.

Sprinkle crushed fried onions, coriander leaves, lime juice and milk over the rice.

Lastly pour the ghee over the rice, seal the pan and cook on medium heat for 35 minutes or till done.

For Tempering
2 bay leaves
5-cm cinnamon stick
2 cloves
2 cardamoms
2 petals mace

RAW MANGO YOGHURT RICE

It's the perfect finish to every meal! On every South Indian dining table will sit the 'curd rice' with a lovely tempering of red chillies, curry leaves and dals. Bits of chopped raw mango add a peppy note to this simple dish.

COOKING TIME: 30 MIN. | SERVES: 4

1 cup rice (not basmati)	Slice the ginger thinly, break the red and green chillies.
2 cups yoghurt	Wash and cut the mango into small cubes; you can remove the skin if needed.
1 cup milk	Cook the rice till it becomes very soft.
1-inch ginger	Add yoghurt and milk and mash well by using a ladle to make sure there are no lumps.
¼ tsp mustard seeds	Heat the oil and add mustard seeds, sliced ginger, red chillies, green chillies, curry leaves, carom seeds, salt and sauté well.
3 green chillies	Add to the rice and mix well.
¼ tsp carom seeds	Garnish with coriander leaves.
3 dry red chillies	
1 big raw mango	
1 tbsp oil for seasoning	
a few curry leaves	
a few coriander leaves (optional)	
salt to taste	

Ingredients:
- 1 cup rice (not basmati)
- 2 cups yoghurt
- 1 cup milk
- 1-inch ginger
- ¼ tsp mustard seeds
- 3 green chillies
- ¼ tsp carom seeds
- 3 dry red chillies
- 1 big raw mango
- 1 tbsp oil for seasoning
- a few curry leaves
- a few coriander leaves (optional)
- salt to taste

Method:
- Slice the ginger thinly, break the red and green chillies.
- Wash and cut the mango into small cubes; you can remove the skin if needed.
- Cook the rice till it becomes very soft.
- Add yoghurt and milk and mash well by using a ladle to make sure there are no lumps.
- Heat the oil and add mustard seeds, sliced ginger, red chillies, green chillies, curry leaves, carom seeds, salt and sauté well.
- Add to the rice and mix well.
- Garnish with coriander leaves.

Note:
Grated raw mango, pomegranate seeds, thinly sliced cucumber, seedless grapes (black and green) and thinly sliced carrots can be used as garnish. Fresh cream also gives it a different taste.

PRAWN BIRYANI

Unlike the other biryanis, in this one the prawns, masalas and rice are mixed together before settling down to cook until done. There is practically no marination, yet this is a heavenly tasting biryani which I highly recommend.

COOKING TIME: 40 MIN. | SERVES: 4–6

2 cups biryani rice
500 gm medium-sized prawns
1 tbsp ginger–garlic paste
1 tsp garam masala
2 tbsp red chilli powder
4 tbsp ghee
2 big onions
1-inch cinnamon stick
3 cloves
3 cardamoms
2 bay leaves
8 green chillies
3 tomatoes
a few coriander leaves
a few mint leaves
salt to taste

Wash and devein the prawns.

Chop the onions finely.

Grind the green chillies, coriander and mint leaves into a paste.

Wash and chop the tomatoes, break the bay leaves.

Wash and cook the rice till it is three-fourths done, remove and drain and keep aside.

Heat the ghee in a deep dish, add the chopped onions, ginger–garlic paste and sauté well.

Add the chopped tomatoes and the green masala paste and sauté.

Add the red chilli powder and whole masala and sauté.

Add the prawns, sauté for a few minutes.

Add the semi-cooked rice, mix well.

Cover and cook on low flame for 10 minutes.

Serve with raita.

COCONUT RICE

Cardamoms, cinnamon and cumin seeds add an eclectic fragrance and flavour to the rice. You can serve it alongside any curry but it tastes best when served with mutton kurma or chicken kurma.

PREP TIME: 10 MIN. | COOKING TIME: 15 MIN. | SERVES: 4–6

2 cups parboiled rice
10 cashew nuts
1 cup grated coconut
1 cup coconut milk
1 tsp clarified butter or butter
salt to taste

For Seasoning
¼ tsp fennel seeds
2 broken bay leaves
½-inch cinnamon stick
2 cardamoms
2 tsp clarified butter
7 slit green chillies
1 tsp coconut oil (optional)
10 curry leaves

Roast the rice with 1 tsp clarified butter, then add 1 cup water and 1 cup coconut milk. Also add a pinch of salt.

Cook and keep aside.

Heat the clarified butter and fry the cashew nuts. Set them aside.

In the same pan, fry the curry leaves, green chillies, cardamoms, cinnamon, bay leaves and fennel seeds. Add the grated coconut and sauté well.

Then add the cashew nuts.

Add this to the rice and mix well.

Heat oil in a pan, add all the seasoning and sauté.

Now add the seasoning to the cooked rice and mix well.

Serve hot.

TAMARIND RICE

This South Indian favourite, and particularly mine too, is a beautiful mélange of a spicy and tangy taste all at once. It pairs wonderfully with cucumber and yoghurt salad.

COOKING TIME: 20 MIN. | SERVES: 4–6

1 tsp black mustard seeds
1 tsp Bengal gram
3 cups cooked rice
¼ cup roasted peanuts
1 cup tamarind pulp
¼ tsp carom seeds
¼ tsp turmeric powder
6 dried red chillies
1 tbsp oil/ghee
a few curry leaves
a few coriander leaves
salt to taste

Mix the tamarind pulp, carom seeds, turmeric and salt.
Heat oil in a deep pan, add the Bengal gram, broken red chillies, curry leaves and mustard seeds.
Sauté well and cook for 5 minutes.
Add the tamarind pulp, mix and cook for a few minutes.
Add the cooked rice, mix and ensure it is coated well.
Cook for about 5 minutes on low flame.
Garnish with chopped coriander leaves and roasted peanuts.

GREEN MASALA BIRYANI

In my biryani world, this green masala biryani wins hands down. Even the chatter of guests would halt a while to allow the biryani work its magic. My niece Avantika said this of 'Patti's' biryani, 'It's spicy, but not so spicy that it sets my face on fire.'

MARINATION TIME: 3 HRS. | COOKING TIME: 60 MIN. | SERVES: 8

1 kg mutton/chicken
1 kg biryani rice (basmati)
6 boiled eggs
12 onions
6 tomatoes
12 green chillies
3 tbsp ginger–garlic
1 bunch coriander leaves
1 bunch mint leaves
2 cups yoghurt
¼ cup clarified butter
½ cup oil
salt to taste

Whole Spices
4 cloves
6 aniseeds
2-inch cinnamon stick
5 cardamoms
2 bay leaves

Half cook the rice with salt, cardamoms, cloves, cinnamon, bay leaves and clarified butter, drain and cool on a thali. Peel the boiled eggs and cut them into halves.

Grind the green chillies, coriander and mint leaves.

Wash and marinate the meat with yoghurt and ginger–garlic paste for 3 hours.

Chop half the onions into slices and half into fine pieces. Also chop the tomatoes, coriander leaves and mint leaves.

Heat some clarified butter and fry the sliced onions with a little salt till crisp. Keep aside.

Heat the oil, fry the finely chopped onions till golden brown, then add the whole spices. Sauté well.

Add the tomatoes and salt and sauté well.

Then add the marinated meat pieces, with the chilli, mint and corriander paste, stir and mix well. Cook on low flame till almost done.

Add the bay leaves and what's left of the clarified butter.

Mix well and add the cooled rice on top.

Garnish with the eggs and fried onions, finely chopped coriander and mint leaves. Melt some clarified butter and pour over the top layer of the rice.

Cover with a lid and a cloth and let it cook on low flame for 20 minutes.

Serve with raita.

Note:
After sealing the dish, you can put it in a preheated oven for 1 hour on low temperature.

CLASSIC AMBUR-STYLE BIRYANI

This biryani with a mix of potatoes, peas and carrots and bits of meat douched in spices and yoghurt is close to my heart. I was dubbed the 'official taster and tester' and was the only one with permission to check whether the chicken was juicy enough to eat. Do note that it's not one of those quick-fix biryanis and will take time to make but your patience will be rewarded by the experience of a gastronomic marvel and you will thank me for it.

MARINATION TIME: 3 HRS. | COOKING TIME: 60 MIN. | SERVES: 8

1 kg chicken/mutton
1 kg onions
1 kg short grain rice
500 gm tomatoes
500 gm potatoes
500 gm green peas
250 gm carrots
3 tbsp ginger paste
3 tbsp garlic paste
4 tbsp clarified butter
4 tbsp chilli powder
2 tbsp garam masala
2 cups yoghurt
1 bunch coriander leaves
1 bunch mint leaves
2 tsp rose essence
8 green chillies

Whole Spices
1 tsp cinnamon powder
6 cloves
6 cardamoms
8 peppercorns
salt to taste

Wash and par cook the rice with a pinch of salt, drain and spread on a wide plate to cool.

Cut the chicken into 6 to 8 pieces, wash and marinate with yoghurt, salt, 2 tbsp chilli powder, garam masala and ginger–garlic paste for 3 hours.

Skin the potatoes and cut into quarters. Peel the green peas, skin the carrots and cut into moon shapes before cutting them into halves.

Cut 500 gm onions finely and chop the tomatoes into four. Cut the mint and coriander leaves finely.

Slice the remaining onions into fine strips.

Slit the green chillies lengthwise.

Heat the oil and fry the onions till golden brown. Add the whole spices and then add the tomatoes, green chillies, chilli powder and salt. Cook till soft.

Add the marinated chicken and green peas, potatoes, sauté well for about 10 minutes along with the carrots. Sauté more for about 5 minutes.

Add 1 cup of water, cover and cook on medium flame till three-fourths done and dry.

In another vessel, pour clarified butter, fry the thinly sliced onions with a pinch of salt till crispy golden brown. Add the cold rice and the coriander and mint leaves, mix well and keep aside.

Take a large wide-mouthed vessel, layer it with some rice, then layer it with the chicken mixture; continue alternately till the last layer on top is of rice.

Sprinkle rose water, tie a cloth around the mouth of the pot and cover with a heavy lid. Cook on low flame for around 20 minutes.

Serve with cucumber/tomato/onion raita finely chopped green chillies.

Make sure the yoghurt is cold.

NOODLES AND VEGGIES IN COCONUT SAUCE

*Mom learned this recipe from a street food vendor in Malaysia.
We're guessing she sweet-talked him into sharing the authentic recipe with her—that was just Mom!*

COOKING TIME: 30 MIN. | SERVES: 4–6

250 gm noodles
2 cups veg stock
2 tbsp red curry paste
2 tbsp light soy sauce
½ tsp white pepper
250 gm Chinese cabbage
1 cup coconut milk
½ cup coriander leaves
2 pods garlic
2 tsp oil
half medium-sized broccoli
2 carrots
1 stalk lemongrass
1 sliced onion
salt to taste

Peel, wash and cut the carrots into thin strips, thinly slice the garlic and onions, cabbage, make broccoli florets and mince the coriander leaves.

Boil water in a deep pan and add a little salt and oil when it starts to bubble. Add noodles and cook for 5 minutes or till done, drain and set aside.

Add the lemongrass and curry paste and stir fry in oil for a few minutes.

Add garlic, onions and cook over medium heat till light brown.

Add the cabbage, carrots and stir for 5 minutes. Increase the heat.

Add the coconut milk and vegetable stock, salt and white pepper.

Boil and add the broccoli and stir in the soy sauce. Lower the heat and simmer for a few minutes before adding the cooked noodles and coriander leaves.

Serve hot.

CHICKEN AND PRAWN NOODLES

My friends from college narrated the story of this prawn and chicken noodle dish that Mom cooked for them. On a day when Bangalore faced riots and angry mobs were blocking roads in the city, two of my friends were stuck on the roads and came home to Mom's place that was close by to wait for the streets to be safe.
Mom welcomed them and soon had them engaged in chatting laughing and digging into a big wok of these mixed noodles they could never forget.

COOKING TIME: 30 MIN. | SERVES: 4–6

250 gm egg noodles	Boil the noodles in hot water and salt with a little oil, drain and set aside. Wash and devein the prawns. Wash and cube the chicken.
250 gm prawns	
3 tsp red chilli paste	Chop the carrots, onions, spring onions, tomatoes, capsicum and bean sprouts.
2 tbsp red chilli flakes	
2 tbsp dark soy sauce	Pour oil and fry the onions and garlic paste.
1 tsp ginger paste	Add the diced tomatoes and chilli paste. Stir in the white pepper powder, salt, soy sauce and tomato sauce.
1 tsp garlic paste	
½ tsp white pepper	Add the chicken and prawns, sauté for a few minutes. Then add the chopped vegetables and salt. Cover and cook on low flame for 5 minutes.
2 tbsp tomato sauce	
½ bunch spring onions	
1 cup bean sprouts	Finally add the noodles and spring onions and toss well.
3 eggs	Scramble 3 eggs and add to the noodles.
1 carrot	
1 capsicum	*Serve hot with soy sauce/chilli sauce/vinegar mix.*
1 onion	
1 chicken breast	
2 tomatoes	Note:
2 cups chicken stock	For a veggie version, add red, green and yellow peppers and also some Chinese cabbage.
10 beans	
2 tbsp oil	
salt to taste	

SOBA NOODLES

This is Mom's favourite noodle dish—no mistaking that! Many a day we would come home after school to find Mom blissfully digging into a bowl of soba noodles tossed with meat and veggies. Noodle comfort, she called it!

COOKING TIME: 30 MIN. | SERVES: 4

1 packet soba noodles
1 tbsp dry sherry
1 tbsp dark soy sauce
2 tbsp red chilli paste
½ chicken breast
2 green chillies
7 spring onions
2 carrots
3 celery sticks
2 cloves garlic
2 cups chicken stock
1 capsicum
salt to taste
2 tbsp oil

Slice the red and green chillies into thin strips.
Slice the capsicum and carrots thinly.
Grate the garlic. Cut the chicken into thin strips.
Cook the noodles in boiling water with salt and oil until almost done. Drain well.
Heat the oil in a wok. Add chillies, garlic and meat. Add a little salt, red chilli paste, soy sauce and cook until the chicken is almost done.
Add the vegetables and the remaining ingredients.
Mix and stir well. Add the noodles and toss well.
Garnish with spring onions.

PICKLES & CHUTNEYS

Pickles need fresh spices, open terraces and the bright sun—it's no wonder that the process of pickling began almost 4,000 years ago. Every culture in the world has a history of pickling to keep food for a longer period of time. South Korea has kimchi. Germany has sauerkraut. The Nordic countries have a tradition of pickled herring. And India—well, we have way too many to count or list!

Miniature cubes of green mango, chillies of all colours and vegetables in tiny shapes are put in ceramic jars tied with soft cotton cloth laid out on terraces, soaking up the sunrays to process and preserve—pickling is almost a sacred ritual handed down through generations.

That's how we inherited this art in the family. Made from veggies to fruits to seafood, Mom's pickles were rich, spicy and delicious. We don't recall ever seeing any store-bought jars at home.

EGGPLANT PICKLE

Mom always said that making an eggplant pickle was pointless if you weren't going to fry the thinly sliced strips of eggplant first because frying it sealed in its characteristic flavours and ensured that there was more complexity in taste to the pickle than just a combination of masalas and vinegar. The result was fabulous and our phone rang off the hook with requests for her to make a 'little extra' for her extended family. And whilst it is best enjoyed with lemon rice or curd rice, I must mention how bowlfuls of the pickle were served as midnight snacks when we were up all night studying for our exams.

1 kg eggplants (medium to large)
250 gm green chillies
250 gm fenugreek seeds
100 gm mustard seeds
250 gm garlic
6 tsp chilli powder
50 gm cumin powder
2 cups white vinegar
½ cup sugar
1 cup oil

Wash and dry the eggplants and cut them into small thin strips.

Slice the garlic and slit the green chillies.

Grind all the masalas with a little vinegar into a smooth paste.

In a big pot, heat oil and fry the eggplants. Remove and set them aside.

In the same oil add garlic, green chillies, the ground masala, salt and sugar. Sauté well.

Add the fried eggplants, some vinegar and cook for 20 minutes.

Serve with lemon rice or curd rice.

Note:
Instead of green chillies, red chillies can also be used.

GREEN CHILLI PICKLE IN MUSTARD OIL

This is a quick and easy recipe with mustard that gives the pickle its pungent, spicy tanginess. The marination process is important in this case so that the shelf life of the pickle is extended by a few months.

It pairs brilliantly as a condiment with simple meals like dal rice, curd rice, vegetable pulao, veggies and roti. We would make a meal out of Mom's chilli pickle and pakoras, stuffed parathas or plain parathas.

250 gm big green chillies
60 gm black mustard powder
1 cup mustard oil
1 tsp turmeric powder
salt to taste

Wash and chop the green chillies. Sprinkle salt and put them aside for 3 hours in the sun.

Heat the mustard oil till it's smoking and then cool it to room temperature.

Add the green chillies, turmeric, mustard powder and salt to taste. Mix well and store the mixture in a glass jar.

Leave it in the sun for 5 days to marinate.

FISH PICKLE

Lime juice, cumin seeds, fenugreek seeds and curry leaves are used in this recipe so their characteristic flavours seep into the fish easily. The addition of poppy seeds and dal give the pickle a denser consistency to go with rotis, bread or steamed rice and dal.

500 gm boneless fish (any white fish like seer or king)
100 gm mustard seeds
100 gm fenugreek seeds
50 gm cumin seeds
50 gm poppy seeds
2 tbsp chilli powder
3 tbsp green gram
1 tsp turmeric
½ cup white vinegar
½ cup oil/mustard oil
2 pods garlic
2-inch ginger piece
10 dry red chillies
8 green chillies
a few curry leaves
salt to taste

Wash and pat the fish dry. Mix chilli and turmeric powder with a little lime juice and rub on to the fish. Set it aside for 1 hour.

Roast the dry red chillies, fenugreek seeds, mustard seeds, green gram, cumin seeds and poppy seeds.

Cool and grind to a smooth paste with ginger and garlic, green chillies and vinegar.

Heat the oil and fry the fish. Set aside.

In the same oil add the curry leaves and the ginger–garlic masala.

Sauté the ground masala well and add salt to taste.

Add to taste fish, vinegar and cook well.

FISH PICKLE IN MUSTARD OIL

Piquant, sweet and tangy at the same time, pickles can liven up some meals and add drama to others. It was the seer fish that found favour with Mom because its meaty pieces wouldn't get mushy when they were cut. Marinated in spices and jaggery and then immersed in mustard oil, the flavours of the fish spring to life in the process.

400 gm boneless seer fish
4 tbsp vinegar
3 tbsp mustard seeds
1 tsp turmeric powder
4 tbsp red chilli powder
100 gm jaggery powder
4 pods garlic
1 cup mustard oil
salt to taste

Wash and cut the fish into medium-sized pieces. Rub salt, and some of the turmeric and chilli powder on the pieces and set aside for 10 minutes.

Heat mustard oil and deep fry the fish pieces a few at a time till all are cooked but not crispy. Set aside to cool.

Dissolve the jaggery in vinegar.

Peel the garlic pods and grind with mustard seeds.

Heat the oil, add balance chilli and turmeric powder, and the ground garlic and mustard seeds.

Mix all the spices with the jaggery paste and the fish.

Let the spices and oil blend into the fish for at least 1 hour and the pickle is ready. The flavours will be richer when left for a longer time.

CAULIFLOWER, CARROT AND TURNIP PICKLE

Our brother ate copious amounts of this vegetable pickle with his sambar and rice. I would sometimes tell him the pickle was over just to enjoy the sight of his crestfallen face light up again as soon as he found it.

250 gm red chilli powder
100 gm black mustard seeds
500 gm jaggery
500 gm tamarind
1 litre mustard oil
1 bottle white vinegar
1 kg cauliflower
1 kg carrots
1 kg turnips
500 gm onions
250 gm ginger
250 gm garlic
250 gm salt

Wash and peel all the cauliflower, carrots and turnips and cut evenly.
Boil for about a minute, drain the water and pat them dry.
Coarsely grind the mustard seeds and set aside.
Grind the onion, ginger and garlic into a fine paste.
Mix this paste with salt, red chilli powder and oil in a large pan and then add the chopped vegetables. Put them out in the sun for a day.
Meanwhile grate the jaggery and soak it with a little vinegar.
Soak the tamarind with the remaining vinegar and leave both overnight.
The next day strain the tamarind pulp with a fine mesh, mix with the jaggery and then mix this with the vegetables.
Transfer to a jar and place in the sun for a few days.

Note:
To dry the vegetables, place them on a cloth overnight.
Boil the vegetables in 2 pots.
Mustard seeds will take some time to marinate in the sun because of tamarind and vinegar.
If eaten after a day, the vegetables will have a bit of a crunch.

SHRIMP PICKLE

Neighbours, relatives and friends would come a-calling just to take back a share of this legendary shrimp pickle—need I say more!

250 gm shrimps
1 cup oil
100 gm ginger–garlic paste
100 ml vinegar
4 tsp red chilli paste
4 tsp sugar (optional)
6 tsp red chilli powder
¼ tsp baking soda (optional)
5 green chillies
salt to taste

Shell, devein and wash the shrimps, then drain out the excess water. Heat 3 tbsp of water, add the shrimps, add salt and cook on a medium flame till they shrink. Lower the flame and add the ginger–garlic paste, chilli paste and red chilli powder. Add the green chillies and stir. Mix half the quantity of vinegar and cook for a minute. Then add half the quantity of oil and cook for 2 minutes. Add the sugar and stir well. Add the remaining vinegar and oil and cook for about 5 minutes. Remove from the stove and cool before storing in a jar.
To preserve the shrimp pickle for a few months, put ¼ tsp of baking soda in ½ tsp of lukewarm water and add this to the pickle before removing it from the flame.

For Chilli Paste
Soak 20 dried red chillies, 10 cloves of garlic and a pinch of salt in ¼ cup vinegar for 1 hour.
Grind to a smooth paste.

SPICY CHILLI AND TOMATO PICKLE

Hot idlis, crispy dosas, upma, spoonfuls of this spicy and sour tomato pickle, and loud chattering were part of the breakfast scene when we were kids. Once we were done eating, there was a race to see who would reach the pickle spoon and be the first to lick it clean.

500 gm red tomatoes	Wash, dry, take out the pulp and seeds and slice the tomatoes, then sprinkle salt and set aside for 2 hours. Keep the pulp with seed.
7 pods garlic	Soak the tamarind in vinegar and extract a thick pulp. Chop the green chillies, garlic and ginger.
1 tsp cumin seeds	Fry the fenugreek seeds in oil and grind.
½ tsp fenugreek seeds	In the same oil, add tomato juice with the seeds and the tomato pulp. Cook for 10 minutes, add all the spices and cook until thick. Add the tomato slices and cook for 5 minutes till thick.
7 green chillies	Cool it completely and then bottle it.
40 gm tamarind	
½-inch ginger piece	
½ cup vinegar	
¼ cup sugar	
¼ cup oil	
1 tsp salt	

CURRY LEAVES CHUTNEY

In South India, no one cooks without curry leaves. Besides lending a distinct aroma and flavour to the food, they are a rich source of vitamin A, calcium, folic acid and fibre. Dollops of curry leaf chutney with my idlis, dosas and appams often made my day.

125 gm Bengal gram
1 lime-sized tamarind ball
2 bunches of curry leaves
15–20 red chillies
1 coconut grated finely
½ tsp salt (or to taste)

Roast the dal till brown and grind it into a powder. Set aside.
Roast the coconut; when half done add the red chillies and curry leaves.
Roast till completely dry.
Make a paste and add salt and tamarind mix to this paste with the powdered dal.
Store in an airtight jar.

IMPERIAL COLLEGE OF SCIENCE & TECHNOLOGY
LONDON

The Governing Body of the Imperial College of Science & Technology has conferred on

G. Pandarinathan

...of the...

University of Madras
FACULTY OF ENGINEERING

The Senate of the University of Madras hereby makes known that G. Pandarinathan has been admitted to the Degree of Bachelor of Engineering, Electrical Branch, he having been certified by duly appointed Examiners to be qualified to receive the same, at the Examination held in the month of March in the year 1960. He was placed in the First Class.

He passed the Examination with Honours.

...under the seal of the University

DATE AND APRICOT CHUTNEY

This dish was a winner with all the kids because of the combination of sweet and spicy ingredients. Even Dad would often be caught with a bowl of this delicious chutney and a very content smile on his face.

2½ cups dried apricots or dates
1½ cups vinegar
1½ cups sugar
1 tsp salt
½ cup ginger pieces
½ cup green chillies

Soak the apricots/dates for 2 days.
Chop the ginger and the green chillies.
Boil apricots/dates in water for an hour till they soften.
Grind the green chillies, ginger, sugar and salt with the boiled apricots/dates.
Boil the mixture with vinegar until it reaches a jam-like consistency. Cook till it is thick again.
Cool and bottle it in an airtight container. It stays fresh for a month.

INDIAN GOOSEBERRY PICKLE

This recipe is handed down by my grandmother. Amla, as it's called in India, is a superb antioxidant and has tremendous healing properties. I remember my grandmother making it into a pickle and telling us how great it's for the skin. This recipe has some tanginess, heat and sweetness. My mom would make it with her farm-grown amlas.

8 tbsp sesame oil
½ kg Indian gooseberries pitted and sliced in quarters
2 tbsp brown mustard seeds
1 tbsp crushed fenugreek seeds
¼ tsp asafoetida
4–5 tbsp powdered jaggery
3 tsp salt
7 red chillies
3–4 tbsp chilli powder
curry leaves
¼ kg tamarind

Rinse and drain the gooseberries. Pat them dry and keep aside.

Soak the tamarind in hot water for 5 minutes and extract the pulp.

Cook the pulp in a pan to get a thick consistency and keep aside.

Heat the oil in a heavy-bottomed pan. Add the mustard seeds, once they splutter, add the asafoetida and crushed fenugreek, curry leaves and red chillies to it.

Almost immediately add the gooseberries.

Make sure the fenugreek is not burnt.

Add the salt, red chilli powder, powdered jaggery and cook till the gooseberries are soft—about 10 minutes.

Add the cooked thick tamarind pulp to it and cook for 5 more minutes.

Cool to room temperature and store in a glass jar.

Refrigerate for up to 2 weeks and always use a dry spoon to take the pickle out.

RIDGE GOURD CHUTNEY

In traditional Indian cooking nothing is ever wasted, not even the peels and the yummy ridge gourd chutney is proof of that. Chutney can be made with the ridge gourd pulp too but Mom preferred the peel. Rice, rotis, dosa, idlis are chutney is accompaniments for me but here's how I love it—crunching through a thick layer atop a hot buttered toast.

500 gm ridge gourd
1 lime-sized tamarind ball
10 dried red chillies
½ coconut grated
a few curry leaves
2–3 tbsp oil
salt to taste

Wash and remove the skin from the ridge gourd.
Grind the gourd and keep the pulp aside.
Wash the tamarind and extract the pulp.
Heat some oil and fry the ridge gourd skin, grated coconut, tamarind pulp and dried red chillies.
Add the salt and curry leaves, sauté well.
Cook and grind to a smooth paste.

Note:
Don't discard the remaining ridge gourd as it can be made into a delicious poriyal (vegetable side dish).

March 2021

My daughter requested me to write a note on my Nirmala.

Going back memory lane, the first time I saw her was in 1961 in New Woodlands Hotel, Mylapore, Madras. I was introduced this smart, beautiful, warm and jovial young lady, by her parents. We instantly got on very well. Six months later we were married.

At the time of marriage she had no exposure to cooking since she had just finished her education which was mostly in boarding school. And also the fact she was coming from an affluent business family, there was limited opportunity to develop her skill in cooking.

In 1962, we left for London for my higher education and lived in Wimbledon and the need arose for her to experiment in the love kitchen. She took an avid interest in the art of culinery. She persued it by enrolling herself at Cordon Blue.

I remember she enjoyed it immensly. This developed into a passion and took it further, and perfected it over the years. She loved feeding everyone who came to the house, which her to be creative with food.

Her upbringing and place of birth helped her to specialize in the flavours of Malay and Singapore cuisine. Also her close association with her family chef who was from Chettinad, helped in widening her skill for this particular South Indian cuisine. The different houses we lived in various Indian cities which book-ingly made into home wafting with delicious aromas, where by all our friends colleagues and family stopped by to have her food... it was an open house for all.

Another aspect was that She was instrumental in converting barren land near Madurai into a beautiful integrated horticulture farm and also made it enjoyable to her children and grand children. We spent our later part of her life in the farm.

I miss her in complete totality. And its always a vaccum that will never be filled.

And I am also grateful and happy that my daughter has documented and compiled this book. Thus sharing some of hundreds of hand written receipts from my wife

Manikavelu
Madurai.

DESSERTS

*H*alwas made of black rice, semolina laddoos (semolina balls), or any other golden-coloured sweetmeat will sit atop the banana leaf before any other fare as an auspicious start to a many-course South Indian meal. While in most cultures desserts are usually the finishing touch to a meal, in South India we believe in grand openings.

We are a sweet-tooth family (no apologies for that) and Mom pampered us with a variety of payasams that were nutty and nutritious. Diwali and Pongal are those conjunctions in the year when all Indian kitchens are bustling, so naturally Mom's kitchen too came alive with prepping and planning three weeks ahead. We loved being part of the many helping hands, more for gorging on those delicious laddoos and barfis. When the sweets were ready, we would don our new clothes and go around distributing them among our neighbours. Sometimes Dad would drive us all across the city to his friends' houses to share Mom's homemade goodies with them.

On the following pages are a few of her popular desserts that you would love to serve at your gatherings.

ADHIRASAM

It was always the first dessert on our prep list for Diwali as an auspicious start accompanied by the sentiment of an offering. In the olden days, adhirasam was a popular offering to the gods during Diwali puja, both at home and in temples in Tamil Nadu. According to age-old inscriptions, the sweet was first made from rice flour, jaggery, butter and pepper. At the annual festival at the Panchavarnaswamy Temple in Tamil Nadu, an offering of 6,000 adhirasams along with 6,000 vadas is made to the gods. And these are cooked in the temple kitchen between sunrise and 11 p.m. for the prayers that take place at midnight.

The authentic way in which this was prepared was so elaborate that it took about a week to make. The rice was first soaked in water and sun-dried before being ground into a fine powder. Then the jaggery was boiled in water and added to the rice flour along with some powdered cardamom to make a thick dough. Next, it was transferred to an earthenware pot, which was sealed and put out in the sun for 3–5 days, so it could ferment. Once that was done, small balls of the dough would be taken and flattened using one's fingers on a small piece of oil-brushed banana leaf and then the dough would be deep fried until golden brown. Finally, the adhirasams would be pressed with a flat-bottomed bowl to remove the excess oil and devoured.

I have skipped the ultra-long prep process to make amazing adhirasams in a jiffy (twenty-four hours compared to a week may be considered quite a victory).

1 kg raw rice	Wash and soak the rice for 2 hours, spread it on a cloth and set it to dry for about 1 hour till it is semi-dry. (The rice should have moisture content.)
500 gm jaggery	
cardamom powder of roughly 3 cardamoms	Grind the semi-wet rice coarsely.
2 tsp sesame seeds	Mix the cardamom powder and sesame seeds to it. Mix well.
5 tbsp ghee/oil	Melt the jaggery to a thick gel-like consistency (to test, drop a teaspoon of it into cold water—it should sink, not dissolve). If you pass this stage, the ball will become hard and adhirasams will also become hard.

Add the rice flour and keep stirring well without any lumps. Transfer the mix into an airtight container and keep at room temperature for a day or refrigerate to last for a week.

Make small flat rounds coated with clarified butter.

Heat oil and fry till golden brown.

BLACK RICE HALWA

This Chettinad delicacy known as Kavuni Arasi is delicious, flavourful and healthy. Mom loved to make desserts that were different and from the heart of her homeland and I found this recipe tucked away amongst one of her many handwritten ones.

2 cups black puttu rice
2 cups coconut milk
1 cup ghee
4 cups sugar (preferably powdered)
50 gm cashew nuts chopped
4 cloves powdered
2–3 drops rose essence

Note:
Black puttu rice is also called forbidden rice (in China). It's an old, traditional rice, also called *kavuni* in Tamil.

Soak the rice in water for 4 hours and keep 2 cups of coconut milk aside.

Drain the rice and grind it to a smooth paste with coconut milk.

Mix sugar with 1 cup of water, add it to the rice paste.

Place this mix over the flame and keep stirring till it begins to thicken.

Add ghee, a little at a time, till the mixture leaves the side of the pan and forms a thick lump.

Add chopped cashew nuts, powdered cloves and rose essence.

Remove from the fire and spread on a plate greased with ghee. Let it cool then serve.

EGGLESS CURD CAKE

I found this recipe of a soft and spongy cake Mom had perfected for my brother and I just had to share it, especially for my vegetarian friends.

1½ cups multi-purpose flour
1 cup thick beaten curd
¾ cup castor sugar
½ cup ghee
1 tsp baking powder
½ tsp soda bicarbonate
1 tsp vanilla essence
3–7 pieces cashew nuts cut into halves
6–7 dates sliced

For Icing
3 bars chocolate
2 tbsp hot water
150 gm icing sugar
1 tbsp butter

Sieve the flour and keep aside.

Mix the sugar and the curd well. Add the baking powder and soda bicarbonate and keep for 5 minutes.

Add ghee and mix well and then add the vanilla essence.

Add cashew nuts and dates to the mix and pour into a butter-greased cake tin.

Bake at 180 °C/ 360 °F for 40–45 minutes.

Method for Icing

Break the chocolate into small pieces and add hot water. Stir to melt the pieces.

Add icing sugar, butter and mix well.

Ice the cake immediately.

Decorate it with gems, silver balls and marzipan roses.

Note:
Use the same recipe for chocolate cake, only substitute 3 tsp of all-purpose flour with 3 tsp of cocoa powder.

COCONUT BALLS

Grate, heat, stir, roll and serve. This simple and delicious recipe is the easiest to make any time. Surprise your family with this quick treat and you can be assured you will be crowned the Dessert Queen.

225 gm khoya
(dried milk used for
making sweets in India)
175 gm sugar
150 gm grated coconut

Place the khoya in a saucepan on low heat.
Stir in half each of the sugar and the grated coconut.
When the khoya gets golden, remove the mixture.
Add the remaining sugar and mix well.
Keep a few coconut flakes in a small bowl.
Make small balls from the mixture.
Roll the balls over the coconut flakes and serve.

This makes about 8 to 10 balls.

JACKFRUIT PAYASAM

Jackfruit payasam takes us back to the two jackfruit trees planted by Mom in our Bangalore home. The large tropical tree with a strong distinct smell can be appreciated from quite a distance. Rich in energy, dietary fibre, minerals and vitamins and free from saturated fats or cholesterol, it makes a healthy summer treat. As jackfruit tree owners we can tell you this fruit requires skill to cut and a palate to appreciate. Soft and sweet jackfruit pieces in milk, garnished with a sprinkling of almonds, melon seeds and a light drizzle of rose water constitutes the jackfruit payasam.

Ingredients	Method
1 big jackfruit	Clean and cut the jackfruit into small pieces.
1 cup sugar	Chop the almonds finely or into strips.
1 cup brown sugar	Boil the milk on low heat till it becomes thicker.
1 cup almonds	Then add sugar and stir for about 15 minutes.
1 cup melon seeds	Add the jackfruit pieces into the milk and cook on low flame for 30 minutes.
½ tsp rose water	
½ tsp cardamom powder	When the jackfruit becomes soft, remove from the stove.
8 cups milk	Garnish it with chopped almonds, melon seeds, cardamom powder and rose water.
a pinch of salt	

BLACK RICE PUDDING

A Chettinad speciality, black rice pudding takes on violet hues that are not just enticing but nutritious too being rich in anthocyanin. Legend has it that this ancient grain was also called 'forbidden rice' because it was once exclusively reserved for Chinese royalty and hence 'forbidden' for the commoners.

½ cup black rice/wild rice	Wash and soak the rice for 2–3 hours.
3 cups water	Boil water, add the rice and cook till three-fourths cooked.
1 cup coconut milk	Add the coconut milk and jaggery.
2 tbsp cashew nuts	Stir well and cook for a few minutes.
50 gm jaggery (to taste)	Lower the flame and cook till soft. Add the cardamom powder.
3 powdered cardamoms	Garnish with broken cashew nuts.

Serve hot or chilled.

DATE CAKE

A moist cake with dates and walnuts makes a nutritious and filling dessert for kids that you can add to their lunch packs too.

500 gm dates chopped	Mix the dates with water and soda bicarbonate and cover and leave overnight.
150 ml water	
½ tsp soda bicarbonate	Preheat the oven to 180 °C or 350 °F.
185 gm butter	Cream together butter and sugar till light and fluffy.
90 gm castor sugar	Add the vanilla essence. Beat the eggs one at a time.
1 tsp vanilla essence	Add half the flour and baking powder and half the undrained date mixture. Repeat the process by adding the remaining flour and then the date mixture alternately.
3 eggs	
215 gm flour	
½ tsp of baking powder	Add the chopped walnuts and pour in a greased baking tray and bake for 1 hour or until the cake is firm.
200 gm walnuts	

SEMOLINA BALLS

Ah! The rich aroma of roasted semolina and the crunch of nuts and dried fruits—a mouthful of happiness that nobody can resist!

2 cups semolina/rava
1 cup sugar
1 cup milk
3 tbsp clarified butter
1 tbsp raisins
1 tbsp cashew nuts

Chop the cashew nuts and raisins, keep aside.
Roast the semolina in a saucepan on low heat till it turns slightly brown in colour.
Add the sugar, clarified butter and milk and keep cooking till the mixture becomes sticky.
Add the chopped cashew nuts and raisins and mix well.
Remove the pan from heat.
Roll the dough into small balls.

Serve when dry.

POLI
Stuffed Sweet Flatbread

Poli is a very popular, traditional sweet flatbread usually made on special occasions and festivals. There are many variations of this recipe but Mom used Bengal gram, saffron, coconut flakes and jaggery to make hers. In fact, she picked up this recipe from the talented cook employed in the canteen at Dad's office.

Sweet polis featured on the menu-du-jour. While it may seem like a time-consuming process, fear not, once you get the hang of it, you'll turn into a sweet-poli-making machine like Mom.

2 cups all-purpose flour	Wash and soak the gram for 2 hours, pressure cook for 6–7 whistles.
2 cups Bengal gram	Drain all the water and grind the dal to a smooth paste without water.
1 cup coconut flakes	Pound the jaggery well and add it to the ground gram, add coconut flakes, cardamom powder and salt as well.
2 cups jaggery	
1 tsp saffron strands	Make dough out of the flour, add a little saffron mixed in water to the dough. Knead well.
1 tsp cardamom powder	
a few strands saffron	Make small balls, roll them out into several thin flatbreads and fill the sweet mixture into the centres.
salt to taste	
water for mixing	Fold all the sides, roll into balls again and flatten with your palm into thin flatbreads.
clarified butter	
	Heat a flat pan, add some clarified butter, put the flatbreads on to it and pan fry on low flame till golden brown on both sides.
	Serve hot and consume within a few days.

Note:
The water drained from boiling dal can be used to make a tasty rasam.

SPICES, STOCKS AND MASALAS

Coconut Milk

1 grated coconut is added to about 2 cups of water. Soak for 5 minutes.
Blend in a blender till coconut is ground well.
Strain in a cheesecloth or a fine sieve and collect the first extract in a bowl. The first extract is the thick coconut milk.
Collect and put the coconut residue back into the blender and add 2 cups of water and blend again for the second extract. Repeat a third time. The second and third extracts will be thinner.

Making the Perfect Tamarind Pulp

Soak a small portion of the tamarind pulp in half a cup of warm water for about 10 to 15 minutes. Use more pulp for a stronger taste or less if you need just a hint of tamarind. Swirl the pulp with your fingers or a spoon so that it dissolves evenly in water. Then strain the mixture with a filter or a sieve before using it for cooking. Mother always used a thin muslin cloth as a filter.

Madras Curry Powder

Ingredients
6 tbsp cumin seeds
6 tbsp coriander seeds
4 tbsp peppercorns
2 tbsp fennel seeds
2 tbsp black mustard seeds
5-inch cinnamon bark
4 bay leaves
3 tbsp fenugreek seeds
2-star anise
20 curry leaves
15 cardamoms
2 tbsp turmeric powder
6–8 red chillies

Method
Roast each ingredient individually as each spice roasts at a different pace until the fragrance is released. In a dry frying pan add the curry leaves till lightly browned. Cool all ingredients and grind together to a fine powder.
Add turmeric and chilli powder. Store in an airtight jar (stays well up to 3 months).

Theeyal Masala

(Roasted coconut with spices)
Roast the following ingredients and grind to a paste. When prepared without the coconut and sambar onions it can be stored in an airtight bottle for a year.
1 tbsp coriander seeds
1 tbsp cumin seeds
½ tsp turmeric powder
1 tsp fenugreek seeds
½ grated coconut
20 peppercorns
5 dried red chillies
10 sambar (small) onions

Garam Masala

Ingredients
20 gm cinnamon
6 gm black cardamoms
50 gm coriander seeds
6 gm cloves
10 gm cumin seeds

Method
Sun-dry all the ingredients for 2 days or oven-dry them. Dry roast each spice separately till the aromas come out. Then grind the spices together. Store in an airtight container. Shelf life is a month.

SPICES, STOCKS AND MASALAS

Clarified Butter (Ghee)

Melt butter in a heavy-bottomed pan over low heat till the butter froths and turns clear after the sediments settle down. Skim off any impurities from the top. Remove the pan from the heat and without disturbing the sediments pour the ghee into a dish.

White Sauce

Ingredients
1½ tbsp all-purpose flour
2 cups of milk
1 tsp pepper powder
1 tbsp butter
4 tbsp grated cheese
salt to taste

Method
In a saucepan over medium heat melt the butter, add the flour and stir well till the butter and flour are combined well. Pour in milk and keep stirring till it thickens. Add more milk according to the desired consistency.
Add the pepper and the grated cheese.

Chicken Stock

Ingredients
bones from a large chicken
1 onion cut in half
2 carrots chopped in 3 pieces
2 celery stocks chopped in 3 pieces
6–8 parsley sprigs
10 peppercorns
8–9 cups water
salt to taste

Method
Place chicken bones and chicken pieces if any in a pot. Add all other ingredients and boil. Add salt.
Bring to a boil and let it simmer for 2 hours. Remove large bones and pieces and strain.
Cool and store in an airtight container in the fridge for 5–6 days or in the freezer for 2 months.

Yoghurt

Take a litre of boiled milk and cool to room temperature. Add a teaspoon of yoghurt or juice of one lime into the milk. Stir gently, cover and leave overnight. Once set, refrigerate.

Memories of Nirmala

So many memories of Nirmala flood my mind, it's difficult to know just when and where to begin. Before she even met me, she had befriended my daughter Nirupa, a friend of Pressy's at Uni providing Nirupa with a home from home in Bangalore for which deed she had my eternal gratitude and appreciation. One day when Nirupa called me from Nirmala's home, long before I had met her, she spoke to me and invited me for a holiday. On subsequent visits to Bangalore, I spent many hours there with her and she took me sightseeing all over Bangalore and to Mysore too. Later on, I stayed with her on all my visits. She gave up her room for me and was always at my side, whenever I needed company.

The first sounds I heard every morning as I woke up were of Nirmala in her kitchen. She had plenty of household staff, but always did the actual cooking herself. I found that her preparations began with grinding a mixture of garlic, ginger and onions which served as a base for her cooking. She also had ground tomato, another mixture of cloves, cinnamon and cardamoms, yet another of mint leaves, of coriander leaves. She was expert at both Western and International cookery and had been trained in London in this cuisines. Her long years in Singapore before marriage had also equipped her with a knowledge of cookery of that region. Nirmala was definitely the uncrowned Queen of her kitchen, where she seemed happiest. I would sit by her watching her, fascinated with her expertise in this department. There was something intrinsically reassuring and comforting about watching her, swift in action and talking as she cooked. She enjoyed digesting ideas and thoughts about the lives of others and cared desperately about the happiness and well-being of her family and friends.

Nirmala was a perfectionist in her crafts and talents and each moment that she spent devoted to that goal was time well spent. Fanfare, flourish and quality were adhered to in every sense. She was a firm believer that traditions must be maintained at any cost and that one mustn't step out of and away from the gallant history of family customs and traditions. She insisted that her children and grandchildren must be endowed with a sense of history. She also loved to shop and introduced me to all the shops where she was a familiar face and bargained for me, seeing that I was not overcharged; took me to her tailors to make my clothes. In spite of her culinary expertise she enjoyed eating out at restaurants and took me to several in Bangalore.

Something I recall with special love is that when my late husband had to go to Chennai for an operation, she and her husband made a special visit to Chennai to see him. I happened to be with her when he died here in Colombo. She never left my side, till I left for home and never told me of his death, taking care to see that I never overheard the constant telephone calls made by my children to her about this and requesting her to keep the news from me. She kept calling me daily after I returned to see how I was and how I coped with the anguish of his death. She cared for me, as few have done; if ever I stayed with her, she would see that my clothes were washed and ironed, saw that I was comfortable and cared for at all times. She was a true friend, rare these days, and I have never wanted to visit Bangalore after her demise.

Nirmala had a bright mind, boundless generosity, a charming, exuberant personality and her lifelong wish was to share the joy and cheer of her life with others who needed joy in theirs.

Her happiest times were spent with her family and her grandchildren who brought her much joy. She never stopped talking about them and was incredibly proud of their achievements, in their individual walks through life.

Whenever I think of Nirmala, I think of these words by Sir William Temple—"The greatest pleasure of life is love, the greatest treasure, contentment; the greatest possession, health, the greatest ease is sleep and the greatest medicine is a true friend". Loving memories of Nirmala and the wonderful times we spent together will be with me till I join her on that wonderful shore which lies ahead for us all.

Ilica Malkanthi Karunaratne

Afterword

I have known Prasanna or Pressy, as we call her fondly, for many years. We have witnessed each other's personal and professional journeys—the ups and downs, the laughter and the tears—and seen it from very close. While she is easy-going, she is also extremely passionate and assiduous about her work.

Pressy started working on this book six years ago and it has been hard work since. This book is the result of a promise Pressy made to her mother Nirmala—to keep her memory alive through her recipes. It's amazing how she scaled every obstacle to bring this book to life. The result is this little treasure of a book.

Being in different countries for long, I never realized that she had a flare for cooking, particularly her mother's dishes, and what's best about the food is it is simple and uncomplicated, much like Pressy. The ingredients are easily available in most Indian homes, but it was her mother's deft touches that gave a flavourful life to all the recipes.

My son Arhaan and I visited Pressy in New York a few years ago and I honestly don't have words to describe the feeling we had after eating the food. I still remember the delicious sambar, fish curry and crabs that were polished off by me and my son within minutes. That's when I got to know about her mother's amazing recipes.

These soulful recipes have travelled from her mother's kitchen in Bangalore, to Pressy's kitchen in New York and now to my kitchen in Mumbai. Every time we have cooked using the recipes, the result has been as delicious as it has been aromatic. I remember my house smelling of all the lovely flavours and everyone entering the house was automatically drawn towards the kitchen. Among the numerous dishes, a few of my favourites are fish curry, mutton cutlet, liver fry.

They say you eat with your eyes before you do with your mouth. Hence, to capture the true essence of every dish, Pressy has its picture alongside the recipe. While Pressy is an accomplished photographer, she trained in food photography in New York, before picking up the camera to shoot for this book. She has captured some drool-worthy, relatable and authentic photographs of these treasurable recipes.

My Pressy is a dreamer, a believer and I truly believe you have to be a dreamer to archive what she has achieved with her book.

When she told me that she's going to name the book 'Ammi' and discussed the main element of the cover art—the sil batta—tears welled up in my eyes. It's so rooted and so Indian! This is a genuine tribute to each and every mother who cooks for their families, with love and affection. The recipes not only move you but also create a connection that will make you keep coming back for more. The recipes are tempered with precision, mixed with affection and peppered with a dash of smile.

Ammi is a warm hug for your soul. This is food made with love for your loved ones.

MALAIKA ARORA

Acknowledgements

Bringing this book to life started with a promise to my mother. It was a journey on its own; on a personal note there was a deeper level of connection of love, respect, healing and understanding of my mother's passion and her life experiences, and professionally this led me to food photography, which I thoroughly enjoy now.

Doing this book was much harder than I imagined and also more rewarding than I thought. In this beautiful and fulfilling journey I want to thank the many people who truly encouraged, supported and helped me make this a reality.

My utmost gratitude to **my Father**, whose advice, help and being there for me gave all the encouragement needed to finish this book Love to **my whole family** who bared their hearts and precious parts of their lives. **Sanjit, Anush** and especially **my niece Avantika** who so happily and lovingly shared many of her memories with me.

My sisters Kavitha Pandarinathan and Anitha Lazar who let me in on my mother's culinary nuances that they possess now.

Chef Charles of *One World, One Kitchen* in New York City for cooking so many dishes to perfection in his beautiful home in Brooklyn.
Sagayam Lawrence for creating and helping bring these recipes to life.
Kavita Santosh for artistically styling the food for so many recipes and the cover.
Sam Mohan for the gorgeous cover photograph and for all his love and encouragement for the book.
Kanishka Sharma and **Himanshu Dimri** for their support.
My dearest friend and college mate **Bhavana Maney** for helping me transfer my thoughts and memories to paper and skilfully writing with all her heart.
Vera Desai for her help in putting this work together.
Sheetal Parakh for beautifully and creatively designing my book and for the enormous patience in tirelessly working on it despite her busy schedule.
Illika Karunaratne for penning a heartfelt and touching note on my mother.
Shvetha Jaishankar and **Preeta Sukhtankar** for their invaluable advice and guidance especially when I needed it.
Dibakar Ghosh, editorial director of Rupa Publications, for all the support and advice.
My friends **Mayura Kuttappa, Nikki Ponnappa, Roopa Lobo, Delnaz Daruwala, Vahbiz Mehta** and **Aditi Govitrikar** for being my cheerleaders.
Malaika Arora for her love, support and enormous help and encouragement.

www.ingramcontent.com/pod-product-compliance
Lightning Source LLC
Chambersburg PA
CBHW061126010526
44116CB00022B/2985